Rethinking
Camelot

Rethinking Camelot

JFK, the Vietnam War, and US Political Culture

Noam Chomsky

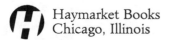
Haymarket Books
Chicago, Illinois

This edition published in 2015 by
Haymarket Books
P.O. Box 180165
Chicago, IL 60618
773-583-7884
www.haymarketbooks.org
info@haymarketbooks.org

ISBN: 978-1-60846-403-6

Trade distribution:
In the US, Consortium Book Sales and Distribution, www.cbsd.com
All other countries, Publishers Group Worldwide, www.pgw.com

This book was published with the generous support of Lannan Foundation
and Wallace Action Fund.

Cover design by Josh On. Cover image of President John F. Kennedy reviewing
the First Air Commando Group at a demonstration at Eglin Air Force Base,
Florida on May 4, 1962. The outfit has trained for guerilla warfare and some of
its members returned from action in Vietnam. (AP Photo)

Library of Congress Cataloging-in-Publication data is available.

Entered into digital printing September, 2022.

Table of Contents

Preface to the 2015 Edition

The immediate occasion for "rethinking Camelot" was the release of a rich collection of declassified documents covering 1961–64, offering a good opportunity to reconsider what I had written twenty years earlier after the appearance of the two volumes of the *Pentagon Papers*, the Gravel edition released by Dan Ellsberg and Tony Russo and the government edition released in reaction.[1] A great deal of other valuable material was also available at the time, and much more had appeared in the interim.

"Camelot" became a favored image of the liberal intellectuals entranced by the years of glory cut short cruelly by the assassination of JFK just at the time when he was about to go on to marvelous achievements—murdered for that reason, according to many admirers. This book is concerned only with what actually happened, which accords poorly with the legend. It touches on the assassination only obliquely, taking no stand on the culprits except negatively: the evidence is overwhelming that it was not a high-level plot with significant policy consequences.

The main focus here is on Vietnam. A core part of the Camelot myth is that Kennedy was planning to end the war. The primary evidence presented consists of two classified documents, NSAM 263 (October 11, 1963) and 273 (shortly after the assassination). These are discussed in chapter 2. The former, in particular, continues to be subject to fanciful misreadings. It is

actually quite clear and explicit, and even though the text was
not available at the time, the press reported its contents accurately. The document expresses the President's reluctant acquiescence to proposals of his advisers that troops be withdrawn if
they are no longer needed to ensure "our fundamental objective
of victory"—President Kennedy's insistent condition, as the
record makes crystal clear, to the day of the assassination.

If Kennedy had had any interest in ending the war short of
victory, he had a perfect opportunity in October 1963, when he
accepted NSAM 263. As discussed in chapter 2, the United
States then learned that the Saigon government it had installed
was seeking a peace settlement with North Vietnam. Washington
could have supported this effort, at least tolerated it, ending the
war gracefully and taking credit for the peaceful outcome, even
claiming in the usual manner that North Vietnam had capitu-
lated, vindicating Washington's noble intervention to defend
South Vietnam from the "assault from the inside" (Kennedy's
term for the internal uprising that threatened to overthrow the
client regime)—"internal aggression," in the interesting phrase
favored by UN Ambassador Adlai Stevenson.

Instead of grasping this opportunity to withdraw with claims
of victory, Kennedy moved at once to crush the threat of peaceful
settlement and US withdrawal, backing the military coup that
installed a regime of hawkish generals more attuned to Kennedy's
goals of military victory.

The newly released information established these conclusions more firmly, as discussed below. Documentary material
that has been released since this book was written makes it even
more clear that the tentative withdrawal initiative was primarily
McNamara's, very likely influenced not only by the belief at the
time that victory was in sight but also by budgetary considerations. In a careful scholarly review, Marc Selverstone concludes
plausibly that "McNamara's effort to devise a carefully cali-

brated, phased reduction of US troops from Vietnam seems to have been a function of federal and departmental planning as much as a response to the war itself."[2]

Selverstone also gently refutes claims about Kennedy's hidden intentions—so deeply hidden that there isn't a particle of evidence for them, though there is plenty of evidence refuting them. But Camelot wish-fulfillment is likely to be as resistant to fact and logic as the rather similar Reagan worship at the other extreme of the political spectrum.

The basic conclusions remain. By the late Eisenhower years, the vicious repression of the regime the United States imposed on South Vietnam in violation of the Geneva agreements of 1954 (which the United States rejected) had finally elicited indigenous resistance, which the regime was unable to contain. Kennedy therefore sharply escalated the US intervention to direct aggression, with extreme brutality: directing US air force attacks (under South Vietnamese markings), authorizing napalm and chemical warfare to destroy crops and livestock, initiating population removal to virtual concentration camps where the population was "protected" from the guerrillas that US intelligence and province advisers knew they were mostly supporting.

Reports from the US military were relatively "optimistic," indicating that aggression might succeed, and would therefore be justified. At that point Kennedy's advisers, primarily Defense Secretary Robert McNamara, called for phased withdrawal. Kennedy reluctantly acquiesced, while insisting, to the very end, that there could be no withdrawal without US victory in the war he launched. Easy opportunities for withdrawal were flatly rejected in favor of escalation, to the end. After the assassination, reports from the field finally began to reveal the truth: the US-run war was failing to overcome "the assault from the inside." The same Kennedy advisers, including those later heralded as doves, therefore called for escalation of Kennedy's war.

The war spread to North Vietnam, Laos, and Cambodia, with horrendous consequences, surely the worst state crime of the post–World War II period. The crime is enhanced by the reaction. There is no need to tarry on Reagan's lauding of a noble cause. Much more interesting are the reactions of presidents who can be taken seriously: President Carter's judgment that we owe the Vietnamese no debt because "the destruction was mutual," or the admonition to the Vietnamese by President Bush I—the statesmanlike Bush—that we seek no vengeance for the crimes the Vietnamese have committed against us, and will agree to let them enter the global system that we dominate if they will recognize their duty to put all else aside and devote themselves to the one moral issue remaining from the war: finding the remains of American pilots whom they murdered while those pilots strayed innocently over North Vietnam. As Bush put it, with much media approbation, "It was a bitter conflict, but Hanoi knows today that we seek only answers without the threat of retribution for the past." Their crimes against us can never be forgotten, but "we can begin writing the last chapter of the Vietnam War" if they dedicate themselves with sufficient zeal to the American pilots still missing.[3]

Across the political spectrum, the Vietnam War is regarded as a US defeat. That too is an interesting reaction. True, the United States did not achieve its maximal aims: Vietnam was not turned into the Philippines. But as the record makes clear, the real concerns were quite different. They were one special case of a leading theme of Cold War history. When World War II ended, the United States was in a position of unprecedented wealth and power, and the political leadership developed sophisticated plans for a global system that would conform to the needs of dominant domestic forces within the business classes. Naturally, they were concerned that the system might erode, as happened at once, with what is called "the loss of China" as China declared independence. A "loss," on the tacit and unquestioned assumption that it is ours by right, part of our world system. The "loss of China" quickly became a major factor in domestic US life, including the rise of McCarthyism: "Who was responsible for the loss of China?" Later presidents feared that they would be blamed for "the loss of Indochina," and much else.

Vietnam in itself was not of great significance to the United States. Rather, it was perceived as a "virus" that might "spread contagion," to adopt Henry Kissinger's later terms for Chile's Allende. A constant theme running through policy planning is that successful independent development, even in some tiny place like Grenada, might have a "domino effect." "The rot might spread" to others, causing real problems. In the case of Indochina, a major concern was Indonesia, with its rich resources, and even to Japan—the "superdomino," as it was described by Asia historian John Dower—which might accommodate to an independent East Asia, becoming its industrial and technological center, independent of US control, in effect constructing a New Order in Asia. The United States was not prepared to lose the Pacific phase of World War II in the early 1950s, so it turned quickly to support for France's war to reconquer its former colony, and then on to the horrors that ensued.

The proper way to deal with a virus is to kill it and protect potential victims from contagion. That was done successfully. Vietnam was virtually destroyed: it would be a model for no one. And the region was protected by installing murderous dictatorships. The most important case was Indonesia, protected from contagion by the 1965 Suharto coup, a "staggering mass slaughter," as the New York Times described it accurately, while joining in the general euphoria about "a gleam of light in Asia" (liberal columnist James Reston). In retrospect, Kennedy-Johnson National Security adviser McGeorge Bundy recognized that "our effort" in Vietnam was "excessive" after 1965, with Indonesia safely inoculated.

In later years a combination of Vietnamese resistance and the growth of a mass and active anti-war movement led the US business community to recognize that the war was no longer worth pursuing, and it was slowly wound down, not without horrific crimes.

It is of some interest and significance that the outcome is described as "a defeat." It was, indeed, a partial defeat, but overall a significant victory.

The "defense of South Vietnam" was not the only achievement of Camelot. Another was bringing "the terrors of the earth" to Cuba, in the words of Kennedy's close associate historian Arthur Schlesinger. Kennedy's terrorist war against Cuba, which was no small affair, was a major factor in bringing about what Schlesinger described accurately as "the most dangerous moment in history," the Cuban missile crisis. Kennedy is much lauded for his cool courage in bringing the crisis to an end. The truth, now well established by scholarship,[4] sheds little glory on the Camelot image. At the peak moment of the crisis, when Kennedy's subjective assessment was that the probability of nuclear war was 1/3 to 1/2, he decided to reject Khrushchev's offer to end the crisis by simultaneous public withdrawal of Soviet missiles from Cuba and US missiles from Turkey—obsolete missiles for which a withdrawal order had already been given because they were being replaced by far more lethal and threatening Polaris submarines. Luckily, Khrushchev accepted the humiliation.

There is much more, some of it reviewed in the final chapter. To quote:

> One of the most significant legacies left by the Administration was its 1962 decision to shift the mission of the Latin American military from "hemispheric defense" to "internal security," while providing the means and training to ensure that the task would be properly performed. As described by Charles Maechling, who led counterinsurgency and internal defense planning from 1961 to 1966, that historic decision led to a change from

toleration "of the rapacity and cruelty of the Latin American military" to "direct complicity" in "the methods of Heinrich Himmler's extermination squads."

That hideous chapter in the history of Latin American travail for five hundred years—now mercifully coming to an end, in significant measure—was brought to a peak of fury by Reagan's terrorist wars in Central America. These ended immediately after the fall of the Berlin Wall with the assassination of six leading Latin American intellectuals, Jesuit priests, by an elite unit of the US-trained and -armed Salvadoran army, fresh from renewed training at the John F. Kennedy school of counterinsurgency, under the direct orders of the Salvadoran High Command. The twenty-fifth anniversary passed in the usual silence accorded to our own crimes. But the facts are not obscure. Genuine scholarship is well aware that from 1960 until "the Soviet collapse in 1990, the numbers of political prisoners, torture victims, and executions of nonviolent political dissenters in Latin America vastly exceeded those in the Soviet Union and its East European satellites. In other words, from 1960 to 1990, the Soviet Bloc as a whole was less repressive, measured in terms of human victims, than many individual Latin American countries,...an unprecedented human catastrophe" in Central America alone, culminating in the Reagan-Bush years.[5]

Apart from the intrinsic importance of the events themselves, the comparison of image and reality, as is often the case, offers a useful opportunity for self-examination.

Introduction
Contours and Context

The chapters that follow deal with a crucial moment of modern history, the escalation of the US war in Vietnam from state terror to aggression from 1961 through 1964, setting the stage for the far more destructive assault that followed. They were intended for another book, *Year 501: The Conquest Continues*, which is concerned with central themes of the 500-year European conquest of the world that was commemorated on October 12, 1992 and the forms they are likely to assume in the coming years. The war planning for Indochina illustrates rather clearly some leading features of the Columbian era. It could be regarded as a kind of case study, one of unusual interest and import. Nevertheless, the material seemed special enough to warrant separate treatment. To keep this discussion more or less self-contained, I will sketch some of the relevant context, in part taken from *Year 501*.[1]

Apart from the terrible consequences for the region itself, the Indochina wars had a considerable impact on world order and the general cultural climate. They accelerated the breakdown of the post-World War II economic system and the shift to a "tripolar" global economy; and the internationalization of that economy, along with its corollary, the extension of the two-tiered Third World social model to the industrial societies themselves as production is shifted to high-repression, low-wage areas. They also contributed materially to the cultural revival of the 1960s, which has since extended and deepened. The notable improvement in the moral and cultural climate was a factor in the "crisis of democracy"—the technical term for the threat of democracy—that so dismayed elite opinion across the spectrum, leading to extraordinary efforts to reimpose orthodoxy, with mixed effects.

One significant change, directly attributable to the Indochina war, is a growing popular reluctance to tolerate violence, terror, and subversion. There was no protest or concern when the US was running a murderous terror state in South Vietnam in the 1950s, or when Kennedy escalated the violence to outright aggression in 1961-1962, or when he and his successor stepped up the attack against the civilian population through 1964. If the President wanted to send the US air force to bomb villages in some far-off land, to napalm people who were resisting the US attack or happened to be in the way, to destroy crops and forests by chemical warfare, that was not our concern. Kennedy's war aroused little enthusiasm, a factor in high-level planning as we will see, but virtually no protest. As late as 1964, even beyond, forums on the war were often—literally—in someone's living room, or in a church with half a dozen people, or a classroom where a scattered audience was assembled by advertising talks on the situation in Vietnam and several other countries.

The press supported state violence throughout, though JFK regarded it as an enemy because of tactical criticism and grumbling. Much fantasy has been spun in later years about crusading journalists exposing government lies; what they exposed was the failure of tactics to achieve ends they fully endorsed. The *New York Times*, expressing the conventional line, explained that the US forces attacking South Vietnam were leading "the free world's fight to contain aggressive Communism" (Robert Trumbull), defending South Vietnam "against proxy armies of Soviet Russia" just as the French colonialists had sought to defend Indochina from "foreign-inspired and supplied Communists" (Hanson Baldwin). The US army and its client forces sought to "resist" the Vietcong, southern peasants who "infiltrate" into their own homes and are "trying to subvert this country" in which they live (David Halberstam), enjoying more popular support than George Washington could claim, as government specialists ruefully conceded. Kennedy's brutal strategic hamlet program, which aimed to drive millions of peasants into concentration camps, was a praiseworthy effort to offer them "better protection against the Communists"—local people whom they generally supported—marred only by flaws of execution (Homer Bigart). Such methods having failed, President Johnson decided in early 1965 "to step up resistance to Vietcong infiltration in South Vietnam" (Tom Wicker)—the Vietcong being South Vietnamese, as recognized on all sides. To the end (indeed, to the present), the media reflexively adopted the framework of government propaganda, tolerating even the most outlandish fabrications and absurdities. Exceptions did exist, but they were rare.[2]

As President Johnson sharply increased the attack against South Vietnam in early 1965, also extending the bombing to the North and introducing US combat forces, there were stirrings of protest, though they were limited and aroused bitter antagonism. Take Boston, perhaps the center of US liberalism. The first public protest against the war was in October 1965 on the Boston Common, with a huge police presence. It was violently disrupted by counterdemonstrators. The media angrily denounced the audacity of those who had sought to voice (embarrassingly timid) protests, but were fortunately silenced; not a word could be heard above the din. The next major public event was scheduled for March 1966, when hundreds of thousands of US troops were rampaging in South Vietnam. The organizers decided to hold meetings in churches, to reduce the likelihood of violence. The churches were attacked and defaced while police stood calmly by—until they too came under the barrage. In suburban towns, mothers and children were pelted and abused when they stood silently in protest against the escalating war. It was not until late 1966 that the climate began to shift.

By the late 1960s much of the public was opposed to the war on principled grounds, unlike elite sectors, who kept largely to "pragmatic" objections of cost (to us). This component of the "crisis of democracy" was considered severe enough to merit a special designation—the "Vietnam syndrome," a disease with such symptoms as dislike for war crimes and atrocities. When Ronald Reagan sought to emulate Kennedy in the first weeks of his term, preparing the ground for a direct attack on "aggressive Communism" throughout Central America, the media went along as usual, but public protest quickly induced the Administration to back down in fear that its more central programs would be prejudiced; press critique of Administration fabrications followed some months later. The Reagan Administration was compelled to resort to clandestine international terrorism, at unprecedented levels, to avoid public scrutiny.

An early Bush Administration National Security Policy Review, leaked on the day US ground forces attacked in the Gulf, concluded that "much weaker enemies" (meaning any acceptable target) must be defeated "decisively and rapidly," because any delay or resistance would "undercut political support," recognized to be thin. Classical forms of intervention are no longer an option, the domestic base having eroded. No more Marines marauding and terrorizing for years as in Wilson's days, or US Air Force planes bombing the South Vietnamese countryside in the Kennedy-Johnson style. The options are limited to clandestine terror with foreign agents, so that the media can pretend they do not see and the public is kept in ignorance; or "decisive and rapid" blows against an enemy too weak to strike back after a huge campaign to portray him as a demon on the verge of destroying us.

Despite some changes, leading themes persist, and merit attention and thought. Naturally there are variations as circumstances change, and the world is far more complex than any brief description of it. Nevertheless, we gain no little understanding of contemporary affairs by placing them in a larger framework of policies, goals, and actions with cultural and institutional roots that endure over long periods.

1. Military Science and Spirit

Adam Smith described the voyages of Columbus and Vasco da Gama, opening up the Western Hemisphere and Asia to European conquest and setting the stage for the devastation of Africa as well, as "the two greatest and most important events recorded in the history of mankind." Writing in 1776, he understood very well the "essential contribution" of these achievements to the rapid development of Europe, and was no less aware that they were "ruinous and destructive" to the populations subjected to "the savage injustice of the Europeans," which brought "dreadful misfortunes." With "the superiority of force" the Europeans commanded, "they were enabled to commit with impunity every sort of injustice in those remote countries" that they reached.

The crucial role of Europe's mastery of the means and culture of violence is substantiated by contemporary scholarship. The inhabitants of Asia and the Western Hemisphere were "appalled by the all-destructive fury of European warfare," military historian Geoffrey Parker observes: "It was thanks to their military superiority, rather than to any social, moral or natural advantage, that the white peoples of the world managed to create and control" their "global hegemony," history's first. "Europe's incessant wars" were responsible for "stimulating military science and spirit to a point where Europe would be crushingly superior to the rest when they did meet," historian V.G. Kiernan comments aptly.[3]

These traditional features of European culture emerged with great clarity in the Indochina wars. There is a direct line of descent from the English colonists who carried out "the utter extirpation of all the Indians in most populous parts of the Union" by means "more destructive to the Indian natives than the conduct of the conquerors of Mexico and Peru" (Secretary of War Gen. Henry Knox, 1794), to the "ethnic cleansing" of the continent, to the murderous conquest of the Philippines and the rampages in the Caribbean region, to the onslaught against Vietnam, Laos and Cambodia.[4]

An indispensable feature of the "military science and spirit" in which European culture excelled, revealed once again in the Indochina wars, is the talent described by Alexis de Tocqueville as he watched the US Army driving Indians from their homes "in the middle of winter," with snow "frozen hard on the ground," a "solemn spectacle" of murder and degradation, "the triumphal march of civilization across the desert." He was particularly struck that the conquerors could deprive people of their rights and exterminate them "with singular felicity, tranquilly, legally, philanthropically, without shedding blood, and without violating a single great principle of morality in the eyes of the world." It was impossible to destroy people with "more respect for the laws of humanity," he wrote.

The more humane thought it advisable to make the savages "happy and useful" so as to save "the pain and expense of expelling or destroying them" (Jefferson's commissioners, preparing the next stage in the near-extermination of the Cherokees, continued under de Tocqueville's eyes, consummated by self-styled "philanthropists and humanitarians" half a century later). "We become in reality their benefactors" by expelling the natives from their homes, President Monroe explained as the groundwork was being laid for Jackson's Indian Removal Act. The perpetrators knew what they were doing, if they chose to know. Secretary of War Knox warned that "a future historian may mark the causes of this destruction of the human race in sable colors," looking askance at the genocidal practices of his countrymen. The "men of virtue" who ran the country also expressed occasional qualms. Well after he left power, John Quincy Adams became an outspoken critic of slavery and policy towards the indigenous population—policies that he described as "among the heinous sins of this nation, for which I believe God will one day bring [it] to judgement." He hoped that his belated stand might somehow aid "that hapless race of native Americans, which we are exterminating with such merciless and perfidious cruelty." But the recantation by the intellectual father of Manifest Destiny and domination of the hemisphere had no effect on the extermination, which continued in full ruthlessness.[5]

Adams spoke from firsthand experience. One notable case, with long-term consequences reaching directly to Indochina, was the "exhibition of murder and plunder known as the First Seminole War,...one part of the American policy aimed at removing or eliminating native Americans from the Southeast," as William Weeks describes General Andrew Jackson's "campaign of terror, devastation, and intimidation" against the Seminoles in 1818 in Spanish Florida, in his study of Adams's diplomacy. The Spanish Minister concluded that "the war against the Seminoles has been merely a pretext for General Jackson to fall, as a conqueror, upon the Spanish provinces...for the purposes of establishing there the dominion of this republic upon the odious basis of violence and bloodshed"—"strong language from a diplomat," Weeks writes, "yet a painfully precise description of how the United States first came to control the province of Florida."

As Secretary of State, Adams had the task of justifying what General Jackson had achieved. So he did, using the opportunity to establish the doctrine of executive war without congressional approval that was extended to new dimensions in the Indochina wars. Adams presented the justification and novel doctrine in his "greatest state paper," as the noted contemporary historian Samuel Flagg Bemis calls it admiringly, a document that impressed Thomas Jefferson as being "among the ablest I have ever seen, both as to logic and style." This racist diatribe, full of extraordinary lies, was designed to "transform the officially unauthorized conquest of foreign territory [Florida] into a patriotic act of self-defense and the United States from aggressor into aggrieved victim," Weeks observes. He suggests that Adams may have been inspired by Tacitus, "his favorite historian," who caustically observed that "Crime once exposed had no refuge but in audacity." Steeped in the classical tradition, the founders of the Republic appreciated the sentiment.

In Adams's version, Jackson sought to defend Americans from "all the runaway negroes, all the savage Indians, all the pirates, and all the traitors to their country" who were mobilized by the British to "wage an exterminating war" against these innocents— a mélange of "half-truths, falsehoods, and powerful rhetoric," Weeks shows. In reality, the aim of Jackson's "bloodthirsty tactics" and aggression in violation of the Constitution was to conquer the Spanish-held territory and exterminate runaway slaves and Indians who had sought to escape the savagery of the colonists—"mingled hordes of lawless Indians and negroes" who were waging "savage, servile, exterminating war against the United States," in the rhetoric that impressed Jefferson and modern scholars. Two innocent Englishmen were executed by the conquerors for conspiring to incite the savages, an act that Adams commended for its "salutary efficacy for terror and example." The story ended 20 years later, Weeks continues, with the "second war of extermination against" the Seminoles, "in which the remaining members of the tribe either moved west or were killed or forced to take refuge in the

dense swamps of Florida," surviving today "in the national consciousness as the mascot of Florida State University." If the Nazis
had been victorious, perhaps Jews and Gypsies would survive as
mascots of the Universities of Munich and Freiburg.[6]

"In defending Jackson," Weeks writes, "Adams was implicitly
defending Indian removal, slavery, and the use of military force
without congressional approval," establishing an important
precedent that holds until today, in the last case.

Extermination of the lesser breeds with utter respect for the
laws of humanity is a pervasive feature of the European conquest. Massacre of people who are utterly defenseless is considered a particular mark of heroism, as we saw again during the
1991 Gulf slaughter. A concomitant is the standard phrase "hero
of X," referring to the manager who sat shuffling papers in some
quiet room while his minions were fighting the battle of X, slog-
ging through jungles and deserts, trying to escape enemy fire, or,
preferably, raining death and destruction from afar. Murder of
infants by starvation and disease through economic warfare, a
US specialty for many years, is considered less meritorious,
therefore concealed by the doctrinal institutions.

The ability to churn out self-acclaim for unspeakable atrocities is highly regarded, virtually an entry ticket to the ranks of
the respectable intellectual culture. The practices are routine,
unnoticed, like the air we breathe. It is, for example, hardly likely
that the producers of the evening news cringe in embarrassment
as they present George Bush in his farewell address, wiping away
a tear as he recalled the US troops who reached out in sympathy
to pleading Iraqi soldiers, thinking perhaps of the "turkey shoot"
on the Basra highway or the B-52 attacks on conscripts hiding
in the sand—or the Shi'ite and Kurdish civilians left to the tender
mercies of Saddam Hussein as Bush returned to support for his
old friend in the interests of "stability" a few weeks later, with
nods of sober approval in news and commentary. And none

would be so rude as to raise a question about the thousands of children dying as Bush and Saddam played their little games.[7]

A related task is to reshape history so as to demonstrate the nobility of our intentions and the lofty ideals that guide us as we bring "dreadful misfortunes" to those lucky enough to fall under our sway. The more hard-headed warn that we should not "revert to form" with the Cold War ended, "granting idealism a near exclusive hold on our foreign policy" as we slip back unthinkingly to our role of world benefactor while ignoring "the national interest"; the world is too harsh a place for us to be guided solely by the "Wilsonian idealism" that has so long lighted our path (*New York Times* chief diplomatic correspondent Thomas Friedman, quoting a high official with approval). This sage counsel also has deep roots. As the country celebrated an earlier victory in 1783, a committee warned Congress not to go to excess in "gratify[ing] their better feelings in acts of humanity"; "generosity becomes bankrupt and frustrates its own designs by prodigal bounty," the committee explained as it recommended the further robbery of Indian lands.[8] The reverential awe over our humanitarian intervention in Indochina, which would fill many volumes, has also been accompanied by regular warning that our generosity might be excessive, possibly harmful to the "national interest."

Falsification of the historical record, often reaching quite impressive levels, can persist for many centuries, as illustrated by the fate of those who faced "the savage injustice of the Europeans" from the early years of the conquest. It was not until the cultural revival of the 1960s that it became possible to confront some of the realities, even in scholarship, apart from rare and largely ignored exceptions.

It would not be fair to imply that the regular fabrication of useful history passes entirely unnoticed. In mid-1992, the *New York Times Book Review* devoted an essay to this abomination, with a lead headline running across the top of the front page reading:

"You Can't Murder History." The thought was jarring, to put it mildly, as the quincentenary approached, with its ample evidence that history can be murdered with the same "singular felicity" as people; the *Times* archives alone provide an instructive record. No need for concern, however. The essay kept to a proper topic: the murder of history in "the old Soviet Union," where history "was like cancer in the human body, an invisible presence whose existence is bravely denied but against which every conceivable weapon is mobilized." The author recalls "those all-powerful Soviet officials whose job it was to suppress the public's memory of this grisly episode" of the murder of the Czar and his family, but who, in the end, "could not hold back the tide."[9]

Unfortunate commissars, whose power base had collapsed.

2. The Deeper Roots

The review of the planning record that follows might be faulted for keeping too close to the surface, ignoring the deeper roots of policy. That is fair enough. Policy flows from institutions, reflecting the needs of power and privilege within them, and can be understood only if these factors are recognized, including the case now under examination.

Every age of human history, Adam Smith argued with some justice, reveals the workings of "the vile maxim of the masters of mankind": "All for ourselves, and nothing for other People." The "masters of mankind" in the half-millenium of the European conquest included Europe's merchant-warriors, the industrialists and financiers who followed in their path, the supranational corporations and financial institutions that are creating what the business press now calls a "new imperial age," and the various forms of state power that have been mobilized in their interests. The process continues today as new governing forms coalesce to serve the needs of the masters in a "de facto world government": the IMF, World Bank, G-7, GATT and other executive agreements.[10]

Institutional structures guided by the vile maxim tend naturally towards two-tiered societies: the masters with their agents, and the rabble who either serve them or are superfluous. State power commonly perpetuates these distinctions, a fact stressed again by Adam Smith, who condemned mercantilism and colonialism as harmful to the people of England generally, but of great benefit to the "merchants and manufacturers" who were the "principal architects" of policy. State policy often incurs great social costs, but with rare exceptions, the interests of the "principal architects" are "most peculiarly attended to," as in this case. The lesson holds as we move on to the modem era, often applying, in an internationalized economy, even after military defeat. Consider, for example, how the interests of the Nazi collaborators in the corporate and financial worlds were "most peculiarly attended to" as the US occupation restored them to their proper place.[11]

In the "new imperial age," trade is increasingly becoming a form of centrally-managed interchange, guided by a highly "visible hand" within particular Transnational Corporations, phenomena of great importance in themselves, which also bear on the ideological trappings. World Bank economists Herman Daly and Robert Goodland point out that in prevailing economic theory, "firms are islands of central planning in a sea of market relationships." "As the islands get bigger," they add, "there is really no reason to claim victory for the market principle"—particularly as the islands approach the scale of the sea, which departs radically from free market principles, and always has, because the powerful will not submit to these destructive rules.[12]

The current phase of the global conquest is described with various euphemisms: the world is divided into "North and South," "developed and developing societies." Meanwhile, the basic contours remain, even becoming clearer as the gap between masters and victims increases, sharply in recent years.

Within the rich societies, the effect has been most notable in the US, UK, and Australia, the three countries that flirted (in limited ways) with the neoliberal doctrines they preach, with predictably damaging results. Internationally, the gap—better, the chasm—has doubled since 1960 in the course of a major catastrophe of capitalism that swept over much of the traditional colonial domains, apart from the periphery of Japan, where standard economic doctrines are not taken seriously and the state was powerful enough to control capital as well as labor. In significant measure, the deterioration of conditions in the South is attributable to the neoliberal policies imposed by the de facto world government while the industrial world pursued the opposite path, becoming increasingly protectionist (notably Reaganite America) in tandem with free market bombast.[13]

Neoliberal theology, to be sure, gets a good press in the Third World. It is highly popular among elites who stand to benefit by policies that enrich them while the general population sink into misery and despair, but don't write articles about their fate. Western ideologues may therefore speak of the grand victory of the doctrines we uphold (for others, rejecting them for ourselves at will).

These processes sometimes yield cheerful macroeconomic statistics, in which case the result is hailed as "an economic miracle": Brazil under the neo-Nazi Generals who took power with the help of the JFK-LBJ administrations is a well-known case. Meanwhile, as the Third World model extends to the rich industrial world, we observe again Smith's lesson at work: wealth accrues to the wealthy and the business press ponders what it calls "The Paradox of '92: Weak Economy, Strong Profits."

Smith's lesson applies directly to the Indochina wars. These are commonly described as an American defeat, a classic case of costly overreach. At the dissident extreme of scholarship and media commentary, well after the corporate world called for the enterprise to be liquidated as too costly, the Vietnam War was finally perceived as a "disaster" that arose "mainly through an excess of righteousness and disinterested benevolence" (John King Fairbank) and "blundering efforts to do good" (Anthony Lewis); hawks took a harsher line, accusing the peace movement, the media, and other criminals of turning what all regard as a "noble cause" into a costly failure.

The costs were real, including the incalculable cost of tens of thousands of American soldiers killed. But a realistic assessment requires the perspective of class analysis that Smith took for granted, as does the business press today, if without his clear-eyed frankness. In 1973, the editor of the *Far Eastern Economic Review* described the US war as a success, which had "won time for Southeast Asia, allowing neighboring countries to build up their economies and their sense of identity to a degree of stability which has equipped them to counter subversion, to provide a more attractive alternative to the peasant than the promises of the terrorist who steals down from the hills or from the jungles at night," so that the region is becoming one of the world's great opportunities for enrichment by "American businessmen" and their Japanese and European counterparts.

Particularly encouraging to such more realistic observers was the "boiling bloodbath" in Indonesia, as *Time* magazine enthusiastically termed it, which littered the country with hundreds of thousands of corpses, mostly landless peasants, eliminating the only mass-based political party and opening the riches of Indonesia to Western plunder. This "gleam of light in Asia" (James Reston, *New York Times*) evoked unrestrained euphoria in the West and much acclaim for the firm US stand in Vietnam, which encouraged the Generals and provided a "shield" to protect them as they carried out their grim if necessary work. Only a shade less gratifying was the military coup that established the rule of the torturer and killer Marcos in the Philippines, and similar achievements in Thailand and elsewhere, "providing a more attractive alternative"—to investors, if not to the peasant—than the social and economic development that was feared in an independent Vietnam.[14]

The US achieved its basic goals in Indochina, though not the maximal goal of duplicating such triumphs as Indonesia. The years that followed have solidified the accomplishment, in a manner to which we return. Coming back to Smith's lesson, though this particular episode of "the savage injustice of the Europeans" may have been costly for the population of the United States, the interests of the "principal architects" of policy were, once again, "most peculiarly attended to."

Throughout history, the rabble have sought more freedom and justice, and have often won improved conditions of life. The "men of best quality" have been less than delighted with these developments. There has been broad agreement among them that the rabble should not be permitted to interfere in the management of public affairs: they should be spectators, not participants, as modem democratic theory holds, kept in line with "necessary illusions" and "emotionally potent oversimplifications" (Reinhold Niebuhr, expressing standard views). As the rabble have gained political and civil rights, it becomes increasingly difficult to control them by force; accordingly, it is necessary to control their thought, to isolate them, to undermine popular organizations (unions, etc.) that might provide ways for people with limited resources to enter in a meaningful way into the political arena. In the United States, these measures have been refined to an unusual degree as a highly class-conscious corporate sector has sought to "control the public mind" in perhaps the world's most free society. The emerging de facto world government offers new means to achieve the long-sought ideal of depriving democratic structures of any substantive meaning. Its decision-making apparatus is largely immune from public interference, even awareness.

"Stability" at home requires that elite elements be indoctrinated with proper beliefs while the rabble are dispersed and mar-

ginalized, and fed their necessary illusions in simplified form. A
significant development of the past 30 years has been the failure
of the doctrinal institutions to achieve these ends. Control of the
rabble can be expected to become an ever more serious problem
as the Third World model extends at home.

3. Keeping on Course

Our "excess of righteousness and disinterested benevolence" in
Vietnam is commonly attributed to the Cold War, the felt need "to
resist every hint of Soviet expansion wherever it occurred, even in
areas that were not vital to our interests," in the phrase that has
grown stale through overuse.[15] The doctrine is not wholly false, but
must be translated from Newspeak to English. The term "Soviet expansion" served throughout the Cold War as a cover for policy initiatives that could not be justified, whatever their actual grounds.

The Indochina wars provide a revealing illustration of the general practice. On deciding in 1950 to support France's effort to
quell the threat of independent nationalism in Vietnam, Washington assigned to the intelligence services the task of demonstrating
that Ho Chi Minh was a puppet of Moscow or Peiping (either
would do). Despite diligent efforts, the task proved hopeless. Evidence of "Kremlin-directed conspiracy" could be found "in virtually all countries except Vietnam," which appeared to be "an
anomaly." Nor could links with China be detected. But all was not
lost. Analysts concluded that Moscow considers the Viet Minh
"sufficiently loyal to be trusted to determine their day-to-day policy without supervision." Soviet expansion is thereby established,
and the formula is available to every sober commentator—though
in retrospect, it is permissible to say that the fears were exaggerated. One of the few really surprising disclosures in the *Pentagon
Papers* was that in an intelligence record of 25 years, the analysts
could find only one paper—a staff paper not submitted—that even
raised the question whether Hanoi was pursuing its national in-

terests, not following the orders of its foreign masters. One can scarcely exaggerate the effectiveness of doctrinal need in enforcing a kind of institutional stupidity.[16]

The actual reasons for terror and subversion, and finally aggression, derive from the basic logic of North-South relations, developed with unusual explicitness in the early postwar period. Recognizing that they held unprecedented power, US planners undertook to organize the world in the interests of the masters, "assum[ing], out of self-interest, responsibility for the welfare of the world capitalist system," as the chief historian of the CIA, Gerald Haines, puts the matter in a highly-regarded study of US policy in Latin America. Each region of the South was assigned its proper place. Latin America was to be taken over by the United States, its rivals Britain and France excluded. Policy there, Haines explains, was designed "to develop larger and more efficient sources of supply for the American economy, as well as create expanded markets for U.S. exports and expanded opportunities for the investment of American capital," a "neocolonial, neomercantilist policy" that permitted local development only "as long as it did not interfere with American profits and dominance." The Monroe Doctrine was also effectively extended to the Middle East, where the huge oil resources, and crucially the enormous profits they generated, were to be controlled by the US and its British client, operating behind an "Arab Façade" of pliant family dictatorships. As explained by George Kennan and his State Department Policy Planning Staff, Africa was to be "exploited" for the reconstruction of Europe, while Southeast Asia would "fulfill its major function as a source of raw materials for Japan and Western Europe," helping them to overcome the "dollar gap" so that they would be able to purchase US manufacturing exports and provide lucrative opportunities for US investors.

In short, the Third World was to be kept in its traditional service role, providing cheap labor and resources, markets, investment opportunities, and other amenities for the masters, with local elites permitted to share in the plunder as long as they cooperate. By the same logic, the major threat to US interests was always recognized to be "radical and nationalistic regimes" that are responsive to popular pressures for "immediate improvement in the low living standards of the masses" and development for domestic needs. Such "ultranationalism" is unacceptable, irrespective of its political coloration, because it conflicts with the demand for "a political and economic climate conducive to private investment," with adequate repatriation of profits and "protection of our raw materials."

An "ultranationalist" regime becomes an even greater threat if it appears to be succeeding in ways that might be meaningful to other poor and oppressed people. In that case it is a "virus" that might "infect" others, a "rotten apple" that might "spoil the barrel." It is a threat to "stability," that is, to unhampered pursuit of the vile maxim. A virus must be destroyed, and surrounding regions inoculated to ensure that the disease does not spread. That may require measures of extreme savagery, which are, accordingly, acceptable or even admirable. The joyous reaction to the "boiling bloodbath" as General Suharto took power in Indonesia in 1965 is a dramatic illustration; the self-acclaim for the bloodbath that the US orchestrated in Central America in the 1980s is another. Examples are all too easy to find. North-South relations, and their ideological cover, quite regularly fall into this pattern.

The Indochina wars are no exception. From the outset, it was understood that "Communist Ho Chi Minh is the strongest and perhaps the ablest figure in Indochina and that any suggested solution which excludes him is an expedient of uncertain outcome" (State Department, 1948). At no point did US planners delude themselves that they had been able to concoct an alternative to Communist-led Vietnamese nationalism; the possibility of a "third force" in the South dismayed them no less, since it too would be independent. Nationalist appeal aside, intelligence warned in 1959 that the US client state in the South could not compete economically with the Hanoi regime, where economic growth was faster and would continue to be, because "the national effort is concentrated on building for the future," not enriching the inheritors of the colonialist legacy. The more general problem was the "ideological threat" of Communism: "the possibility that the Chinese Communists can prove to Asians by progress in China that Communist methods are better and faster than democratic methods," as Kennedy adviser Walt Rostow put it. Adopting this conventional viewpoint, the State Department recommended that the US try to retard the economic development of the Communist Asian states.[17]

In Indochina, the only way to create deprivation and suffering in the North and protect the US client in the South from "the assault from the inside," as Kennedy termed the resistance to his aggression, was to increase violence. Our "blundering efforts to do good" could take no other course, given the circumstances. And as always, the same logic dictated the support for murderous terror states elsewhere in the region, to protect them from the virus. These are standard features of North-South relations, exhibited with unusual clarity in the case of Indochina, but rated X, unacceptable for a general audience.

Extremes of state terror are commonly necessary "to destroy permanently a perceived threat to the existing structure of socioeconomic privilege by eliminating the political participation of the numerical majority...," in the words of the leading academic specialist on human rights in Latin America, Lars Schoultz, describing the goals of the neo-Nazi National Security States that had their roots in Kennedy Administration policies designed to prevent the Cuban rot from spreading. The US client regime in South Vietnam was driven to the same course.

Despite their best efforts, responsible intellectuals often find it difficult to conceal US government support for these measures. That is a problem, because US leaders are benign, humane, committed to democracy and freedom and human rights, and otherwise saintly in disposition, by doctrinal fiat. When their dedication to savage atrocities is revealed too clearly, new devices are needed to resolve the contradiction between truth and Higher Truth. One technique is the doctrine of "change of course." Yes, bad things have happened as we departed from our noble course for unfortunate though understandable reasons; but now it is all past, we can forget history, and march forward proudly to a grand future. Those who cannot manage such routines with a straight face would do well to put aside any thought of a career as a respectable commentator on affairs.

The current variant of this standard device is to attribute the crimes committed by the US and its clients to the Cold War. With virtue victorious at last, we can now return to our humanitarian mission of bringing peace, joy, and plenty to suffering people everywhere. We can garb ourselves again in the mantle of "Wilsonian idealism," though bearing in mind that it's a tough world, with many villains ready to assault us if we do not keep up our guard.

To select an example at random, after Indonesia committed the error of carrying out a massacre in front of TV cameras and brutally beating two US journalists in Dili, East Timor, in November 1991, the editors of the *Washington Post*, to their credit, suggested that the US "should be able to bring its influence to bear on this issue," noting that for 16 years Washington had been supporting an Indonesian invasion and forced annexation that had killed "up to a third of the population." The reasons, the *Post* explained, is that "the American government was in the throes of its Vietnam agony, unprepared to exert itself for a cause" that could harm relations "with its sturdy anti-Communist ally in

Jakarta. But that was then. Today, with the East-West conflict gone, almost everyone is readier to consider legitimate calls for self-determination."[18]

The relation of Indonesia's invasion to the East-West conflict was a flat zero. Unexplained is why, in the throes of its Vietnam agony, the US found it necessary to increase the flow of weapons to its Indonesian client at the time of the 1975 invasion, and to render the UN "utterly ineffective in whatever measures it undertook" to counter the aggression, as UN Ambassador Daniel Patrick Moynihan proudly described his success in following State Department orders. Or why the Carter Administration felt obligated to sharply accelerate the arms flow in 1978 when Indonesian supplies were becoming depleted and the slaughter was reaching truly genocidal proportions. Or why the Free Press felt that duty required that it reduce its coverage of these events as the slaughter mounted, reaching zero as it peaked in 1978, completely ignoring easily accessible refugees, respected Church sources, human rights groups, and specialists on the topic, in favor of Indonesian Generals and State Department prevaricators. Or why today it refuses to tell us about the rush of Western oil companies to join Indonesia in the plunder of Timorese oil. All is explained by the Cold War, now behind us, so that we may dismiss past errors to the memory hole and return to the path of righteousness.

Absurdity aside, the thesis is instantly refuted by a look at what came before the Cold War and what immediately followed it; no change in the willingness to resort to repression, subversion, violence, and terror is detectable from Woodrow Wilson and his predecessors through the Cold War and beyond. The historical record, however, has no bearing on Higher Truths. The thesis stands, whatever the facts; such is the way with doctrinal necessity.

More interestingly, the thesis mistakes the nature of the Cold War, another topic that merits at least a brief look, given its importance for understanding the events of this 70-year pe-

riod—including the Indochina wars from 1945 until today—and
the doctrinal framework that is designed to provide them with
an acceptable cast.

4. The Kremlin Conspiracy

In no small measure, the Cold War itself can be understood as a
phase of the "North-South confrontation," so unusual in scale
that it took on a life of its own, but grounded in the familiar logic.

Eastern Europe was the original "Third World," diverging
from the West along a fault line running through Germany even
before the Columbian era, the West beginning to develop, the
East becoming its service area. By the early 20th century, much
of the region was a quasi-colonial dependency of the West. The
Bolshevik takeover in 1917 was immediately recognized to be
"ultranationalist," hence unacceptable. Furthermore, it was a
"virus," with substantial appeal in the Third World.

The Western invasion of the Soviet Union was therefore justified in defense against "the Revolution's challenge...to the very
survival of the capitalist order," the leading diplomatic historian
John Lewis Gaddis comments today, reiterating the basic position
of US diplomacy of the 1920s: "The fundamental obstacle" to
recognition of the USSR, the chief of the Eastern European Division of the State Department held, "is the world revolutionary
aims and practices of the rulers of that country." These "practices,"
of course, did not involve literal aggression; rather, interfering with
Western designs, which is tantamount to aggression. The Kremlin
conspiracy to take over the world was therefore established, a
record replayed in later years as other ultranationalists and viruses
were assigned to the category of "Soviet expansion."

The industrial West was also thought to be susceptible to the
plague. The Bolsheviks sought to make the "ignorant and inca-
pable mass of humanity dominant in the earth," Woodrow Wilson's
Secretary of State Robert Lansing warned. They were appealing

"to the proletariat of all countries, to the ignorant and mentally deficient, who by their numbers are urged to become masters,... a very real danger in view of the process of social unrest throughout the world." When soldiers' and workers' councils made a brief appearance in Germany, Wilson feared that they would inspire dangerous thoughts among "the American negro [soldiers] returning from abroad." Already, he had heard, negro laundresses were demanding more than the going wage, saying that "money is as much mine as it is yours." Businessmen might have to adjust to having workers on their boards of directors, he feared, among other disasters, if the Bolshevik virus were not exterminated.

It was therefore necessary to defend the West from "the Revolution's challenge" at home as well. As Lansing explained, force must be used to prevent "the leaders of Bolshevism and anarchy" from proceeding to "organize or preach against government in the United States." The repression launched by the Wilson Administration successfully undermined democratic politics, unions, freedom of the press, and independent thought, safeguarding business interests and their control over state power. The story was re-enacted after World War II, again under the pretext of the Kremlin conspiracy.

According to the official version, it was Soviet crimes that aroused Western antagonism. In his scholarly history of Soviet-American relations, George Kennan writes that the dissolution of the Constituent Assembly in January 1918 created the breach with the Western world with "an element of finality." British Ambassador to Petrograd Sir George Buchanan was "deeply shocked," Kennan writes, and advocated armed intervention to punish the crime. The idealistic Woodrow Wilson was particularly distraught, reflecting the "strong attachment to constitutionality" of the American public, deeply offended by the sight of a government with no mandate beyond "the bayonets of the Red Guard."[19]

A few months later, Wilson's army dissolved the National Assembly in occupied Haiti "by genuinely Marine Corps methods," in the words of Marine commander Major Smedley Butler. The reason was that the Haitian legislature refused to ratify a Constitution imposed by the invaders that gave them the right to buy up Haiti's lands. A Marine-run plebiscite remedied the problem: under Washington's guns, the US-designed Constitution was ratified by a mere 99.9 percent majority, with 5 percent of the population participating. Wilson's "strong attachment to constitutionality" was unmoved by the sight of a government with no mandate beyond "the bayonets of the Marine occupiers"; nor Kennan's. Quite the contrary. To this day the events figure in the amusing reconstructions entitled "history" as an illustration of US "humanitarian intervention," and its difficulties (for us). Gone from "history" along with this episode is the restoration of virtual slavery, Marine Corps massacres and terror, the dismantling of the constitutional system, and the takeover of Haiti by US corporations, much as in the neighboring Dominican Republic, where Wilson's invading armies were only a shade less destructive, perhaps because their racist barbarism did not reach such extreme levels when confronting "spics" instead of "niggers."

Accordingly, Wilson is revered as a great moral teacher and the apostle of self-determination and freedom, and we may now consider returning to the heady days of Wilsonian idealism. The Bolsheviks, in contrast, had so violated our high ideals that they had to be overthrown by force.

Following the same high principles, the US enthusiastically welcomed the "fine young revolution" carried out by Benito Mussolini in Italy in 1922, as the American Ambassador described the imposition of Fascism. Well into the 1930s, Mussolini was that "admirable Italian gentleman," in the words of the man who (falsely) took credit for the Constitution imposed upon Haiti, President Franklin Delano Roosevelt. Fascist atrocities were acceptable because they blocked the threat of a second Russia, the State Department explained. Hitler was supported as a "moderate" for the same reason. In 1937, the State Department saw fascism as compatible with US economic interests, and also the natural reaction of "the rich and middle classes, in self-defense" when the "dissatisfied masses, with the example of the Russian revolution before them, swing to the Left." Fascism therefore "must succeed or the masses, this time reinforced by the disillusioned middle classes, will again turn to the left." US diplomat William Bullitt (Kennan's mentor), leaving his post as Ambassador to Moscow in 1936, "believed that only Nazi Germany could stay the advance of Soviet Bolshevism into Europe," Daniel Yergin observes—not, of course, by conquest. The US business world grasped the point. Major US corporations were heavily involved in German war production, sometimes enriching themselves (notably, the Ford motor company) by joining in the plunder of Jewish assets under Hitler's Aryanization program. "U.S. investment in Germany accelerated rapidly after Hitler came to power," Christopher Simpson writes, increasing "by some 48.5 percent between 1929 and 1940, while declining sharply everywhere else in continental Europe" and barely holding steady in Britain.

Similar conceptions are currently being revived by right-wing German historians, who argue that Hitler's invasion of Russia may be regarded as "objectively a preventive war," since "a group of people, whether a class or a *Volk*, that is threatened with annihilation by another group, defends itself and has a fundamental right to defend itself"; "Hitler had good reasons to be convinced of the determination of his enemies [the Bolsheviks and the Jews] to annihilate him" (Ernst Nolte). Parts of this picture may well become the accepted doctrine of the future, given its utility for power interests, though presumably we will not return to the mid-1930s, when Bullitt attributed diplomatic problems to the fact that the Russian Foreign Office "has been purged recently

of all its non-Jewish members, and it is perhaps only natural that
we should find the members of that race more difficult to deal
with than the Russians themselves," in particular a "wretched little kike" whose influence he deplored. We may also anticipate
further reconsideration of the failure to follow through on the
opportunities for a separate peace with Hitler that would have
left the Germans and the Russians to slaughter one another, with
the US and Britain standing back until it came time to pick up
the pieces.[20]

As Gaddis and other serious historians recognize, the Cold
War began in 1917, not 1945. Whatever one believes about the
post-World War II period, no one regarded the USSR as a *military* threat in earlier years, though it was agreed that the virus
had to be contained and if possible destroyed—much the same
policies adopted at once after World War II. By then, the "rotten
apple" had grown to include Eastern Europe, undermining Western access to traditional resources. Its ability "to spoil the barrel"
had also increased, again, not only in the South. The Communists are able to "appeal directly to the masses," President Eisenhower complained. His Secretary of State, John Foster Dulles,
deplored the Communist "ability to get control of mass movements," "something we have no capacity to duplicate." "The poor
people are the ones they appeal to and they have always wanted
to plunder the rich." In July 1945, a major study of the State and
War Departments warned of "a rising tide all over the world
wherein the common man aspires to higher and wider horizons."
Russia's "actions in the past few years give us no assured bases
for supposing she has not flirted with the thought" of expanding
"her influence over the earth" by associating with these dangerous currents. Russia "has not yet proven that she is entirely without expansionist ambitions" of this kind.

Furthermore, the USSR had now become a major military
force. While planners never expected an unprovoked Soviet at-

tack, they were concerned that the USSR might react to the reconstruction of its traditional enemies, Germany and Japan, as part of a hostile military alliance that constituted a severe security threat, Western analysts recognized. That aside, Soviet power was a deterrent to the exercise of force by the US and its allies; and for its own cynical reasons, the USSR often lent support to targets of US attack and subversion, thus interfering with "stability." Its very existence as a major power provided a certain space for nonalignment and a degree of independence in the Third World. Lesser "rotten apples" posed no such dangers.

It should be stressed that Stalin's awesome crimes were of no concern to Truman and other high officials. Truman liked and admired Stalin, and felt that he could deal with him as long as the US got its way 85 percent of the time. Other leading figures agreed. As with a host of other murderers and torturers of lesser scale, the unacceptable crime is disobedience; the same is true of priests who preach "the preferential option for the poor," secular nationalists in the Arab world, Islamic Fundamentalists, democratic socialists, or independent elements of any variety.

If we can extricate ourselves from convenient mythology, the picture in Indochina comes into focus. It was Ho Chi Minh's "ultranationalism" that made him unacceptable, not his services to the "Kremlin conspiracy" or "Soviet expansion," except in the Orwellian sense of these terms.

5. Varieties of Infamy

The quincentenary provided many opportunities to examine "the murder of history," apart from the obvious ones. Some were taken. The 500th year opened in October 1991 with a flood of commentary on the 50th anniversary of Japan's December 7 attack on Pearl Harbor. There was wonder and dismay over Japan's singular unwillingness to acknowledge its guilt for "the date which will live in infamy," and sober ruminations on Japan's disgraceful "self-pity" and refusal to offer reparations to its victims, its "clumsy attempts to sanitize the past," and failure to "come forward with a definitive statement of wartime responsibility," as Tokyo correspondent Steven Weisman framed the issues in a *New York Times Magazine* cover story on "Pearl Harbor in the Mind of Japan." These deliberations were carefully crafted to highlight Japan's major crime: its "sneak attack" on Pearl Harbor. Among the issues scrupulously excised were the US attitude towards Japan's horrifying rampages before the infamous date, and the great power interactions that lie not very deep in the background. And one would have to search diligently for a discussion of the proper rank, in the scale of atrocities, of an attack on a naval base in a US colony that had been stolen from its inhabitants by force and guile just 50 years earlier—another part of the background that slipped by virtually unnoticed, as did the centenary of the latter deed in January 1993.

More remarkable still was another anniversary passed over in silence at the very same moment: the thirtieth anniversary of John F. Kennedy's escalation of the US intervention in South Vietnam. Autumn 1961 was a fateful moment in the history of US assault against Indochina, one of the most shameful and destructive episodes of the 500-year conquest.

On October 11, 1961, Kennedy ordered dispatch of a US Air Force Farmgate squadron to South Vietnam, 12 planes especially equipped for counterinsurgency warfare, soon authorized "to fly coordinated missions with Vietnamese personnel in support of Vietnamese ground forces." On December 16, Defense Secretary Robert McNamara, whom JFK had put in charge of running the war, authorized their participation in combat operations against southerners resisting the violence of the US-imposed terror state or living in villages out of government control. These were the first steps in engaging US forces directly in bombing and other combat operations in South Vietnam from 1962, along with sabotage missions in the North. These 1961-1962 actions laid the groundwork for the huge expansion of the war in later years, with its awesome toll.[21]

State terror had already taken perhaps 75,000 lives in the southern sector of Vietnam since Washington took over the war directly in 1954. But the 1954-1961 crimes were of a different order: they belong to the category of crimes that Washington conducts routinely, either directly or through its agents, in its various terror states. In the fall and winter of 1961-1962, Kennedy added the war crime of aggression to the already sordid record, also raising the attack to new heights.

6. Varieties of Crime

Not all crimes are of the same order; it is worthwhile to distinguish terror from aggression, however academic the distinction may seem to the victims. To illustrate, take a contemporary example, one of those that receives little notice and that demonstrates, once again, the utter irrelevance of the conventional Cold War pretexts served up by the murderers of history when public concern over criminal actions has to be allayed. Consider Colombia, second only to El Salvador as a recipient of US military aid in Latin America. The State Department *Country Reports* for 1990 states that "Members and units of the army and the police participated in a disturbing number of human rights violations including extrajudicial executions, torture, and massacres." "Yet no security assistance has been withheld as a result of widespread violations by aid recipients" (the security forces), Americas Watch comments. In fiscal 1991, Colombia received $27.1 million in military assistance and $20 million in police aid, along with $50 million in Economic Support Funds for counter-narcotics assistance—funds commonly used for repression, with no drug connection, as widely reported. In March 1990, two high-ranking Colombian generals informed Congress that "the generals would use $38.5 million of the $40.3 million originally appropriated for

fiscal year 1990 counter-narcotics assistance for counter-insurgency support in areas where narcotics trafficking was nonexistent," Americas Watch notes, citing a congressional report.

For fiscal year 1992, Colombia was scheduled to receive $58
million in military assistance and $20 million for the police; the
same amount was requested for fiscal 1993. From 1988 to 1991,
US military aid to Colombia increased sevenfold, keeping pace
with atrocities by the security forces. The 117 US military advisers
are more than twice the number allowed by Congress form Salvador (whatever the actual numbers may have been). Over 3,000
cases of abuse by police and military were reported from January
1990 to April 1991, according to a study by the Colombian Attorney General, including 68 massacres, 560 murders, 664 cases of
torture, and 616 disappearances. This is apart from the atrocities
carried out by paramilitary groups that operate with the tolerance
of the government, if not direct participation. As usual in the US-
backed terror states, the major targets are political dissidents,
union leaders, and others who seek to organize the rabble, thus interfering with the service role assigned to the South.[22]

These are familiar conditions of life in US domains; Colombian state terror is beyond the norm, but other clients are expected
to act the same way when circumstances warrant, and regularly
do. In the case of Colombia, the Kennedy Administration escalated the standard procedures, helping establish more firmly the
regime of state terror as part of its general program of reinforcing
the apparatus of repression throughout Latin America.

The background is discussed by Alfredo Vásquez Carrizosa,
president of the Colombian Permanent Committee for Human
Rights. "Behind the façade of a constitutional regime," he observes, "we have a militarized society under the state of siege provided" by the 1886 Constitution, which grants a wide range of
rights, but with no relation to reality. "In this context poverty and
insufficient land reform have made Colombia one of the most

tragic countries of Latin America." Land reform, which "has practically been a myth," was legislated in 1961, but "has yet to be implemented, as it is opposed by landowners, who have had the power to stop it." The result of the prevailing misery has been violence, including *La Violencia* of the 1940s and 1950s, which took hundreds of thousands of lives. "This violence has been caused not by any mass indoctrination, but by the dual structure of a prosperous minority and an impoverished, excluded majority, with great differences in wealth, income, and access to political participation."

"Violence has been exacerbated by external factors," Vásquez continues. "In the 1960s the United States, during the Kennedy administration, took great pains to transform our regular armies into counterinsurgency brigades, accepting the new strategy of the death squads." These Kennedy initiatives "ushered in what is known in Latin America as the National Security Doctrine,...not defense against an external enemy, but a way to make the military establishment the masters of the game...[with] the right to combat the internal enemy, as set forth in the Brazilian doctrine, the Argentine doctrine, the Uruguayan doctrine, and the Colombian doctrine: it is the right to fight and to exterminate social workers, trade unionists, men and women who are not supportive of the establishment, and who are assumed to be communist extremists. And this could mean anyone, including human rights activists such as myself."[23]

The president of the Colombian human rights commission is reviewing facts familiar throughout Latin America. Military-controlled National Security states dedicated to "internal security" by assassination, torture, disappearance, and sometimes mass murder, constituted one of the two major legacies of the Kennedy Administration to Latin America, the other being the Alliance for Progress, a statistical success and social catastrophe (apart from foreign investors and domestic elites).

Under Eisenhower, the acts of the client state in South Vietnam fell within the general category of US-backed state terror.
But in this case, his successor did not simply extend these measures, as he did in Latin America. Rather, Kennedy moved on to
armed attack, a different category of criminal behavior.

The assault that followed left three countries utterly devastated with millions dead, untold numbers of maimed, widows and
orphans, children being killed to this day by unexploded bombs,
deformed fetuses in hospitals in the South—not the North,
spared the particular atrocity of chemical warfare—and a record
of criminal savagery that would fill many a docket, by the standards of Nuremberg. By 1967, the bitterly anti-Communist
French military historian and Indochina specialist Bernard Fall
warned that "Vietnam as a cultural and historic entity...is threatened with extinction...[as]...the countryside literally dies under
the blows of the largest military machine ever unleashed on an
area of this size." After the January 1968 Tet Offensive, the onslaught became even more violent, along with "secret bombing"
of Laos and later Cambodia that added hundreds of thousands
of additional casualties—"secret," because the media refused to
find out what was happening, or to make public what they knew.

The land itself was targeted for destruction, not merely the
people. Extensive regions were turned into moonscapes. The
"unprecedentedly massive and sustained expenditure of herbi-
cidal chemical warfare agents against the fields and forests of
South Vietnam...resulted in large-scale devastation of crops, in
widespread and immediate damage to the inland and coastal
forest ecosystems, and in a variety of health problems among
exposed humans," American biologist Arthur Westing concluded. The effects are enduring. The director of the Center for
National Resources Management and Environmental Studies
at the University of Hanoi, biologist Vo Quy, writes that the destruction of huge areas of jungle left grasslands in which rat

populations have exploded, destroying crops and causing disease, including bubonic plague, which spread in South Vietnam from 1965. Defoliants eliminated half the mangrove forests of the country, leaving "a solid gray scene of death," US biologist E.W. Pfeiffer observed after a visit. Drainage of regions of the Mekong Delta by the US army in counterinsurgency operations raised the sulphuric acid too high for crops to grow. Large areas "that were once cool, moist, temperate and fertile are now characterised by compacted, leached earth and dry, blazing climate," Vo Quy writes, after "deliberate destruction of the environment as a military tactic on a scale never seen before." To "heal the war-scarred country" would be a huge task under the best of circumstances.[24]

7. "Crime Once Exposed..."

In October 1991, President Bush celebrated the thirtieth anniversary of Kennedy's escalation of the war—coincidentally, opening the 500th year of the European conquest—by intervening once again to block European and Japanese efforts to end the embargo that the US imposed in 1975 to ensure that the desperately poor and ruined country would not recover from the "dreadful misfortunes" it had suffered. Presumably there were other reasons as well: to punish Vietnam for its failure to succumb to US violence, to teach appropriate lessons to others who might be tempted to emulate such misbehavior, perhaps simply for revenge. Secretary of Defense Dick Cheney reported to Congress that we are not yet ready to grant the Vietnamese entry into the civilized world. The reason is that, like the evil Japanese, the Vietnamese are still unwilling to face up to the crimes that they committed against us.

The Indochina wars have not been completely erased from historical memory. From the horrifying record, one issue still remains: our suffering at the hands of the Vietnamese barbarians, who, after attacking us in South Vietnam when we were nobly defending it from its population, compounded their crimes by refusing to dedicate themselves with sufficient zeal to accounting for the remains of the American pilots they had viciously blasted from the skies over Vietnam and Laos. "Substantial progress" on the MIA issue is required as a condition for our normalizing ties with Vietnam, Secretary of State James Baker announced, a process that could take several years. "Despite improved coop-eration," the Vietnamese have a long way to go before we end the embargo that has been strangling them, deterring aid and in-vestment from other countries reluctant to step on the toes of the Godfather and blocking assistance from international lending organizations, where the US wields an effective veto.

The message has resounded in a drumbeat of articles and opinion pieces, with scarcely a departure from doctrinal rigor. For years, the Free Press has been reporting US outrage over the deceitful Vietnamese who evade their responsibility for their crimes against us, without a hint that something may be amiss. Not only do we retain the abilities that so impressed de Toc-queville, destroying people with absolute "respect for the laws of humanity," but we have progressed well beyond, converting our tortured victims into our torturers.

Admittedly, this is no innovation; rather, historical practice that goes back to the days when the authors of the Declaration of Independence denounced the "merciless Indian savages" whom they were exterminating and expelling, an act quite readily absorbed into the official culture of self-congratulation. We learn much by recalling the traditional principle that "Crime once ex-posed had no refuge but in audacity."

As noted earlier, that principle may have been in John Quincy Adams's mind when he established the doctrine of exec-utive war that was again implemented in Vietnam. In fact, Adams went a step beyond the portrayal of extermination as self-

defense against "mingled hordes of lawless Indians and negroes."
He knew that Jackson was "a barbarian," as he privately called
him, and that aggression was aggression. As his later confessions
reveal, he also knew just who was fighting an "exterminating
war." But he also knew that the US had the guns; and, following
the principle enunciated by his favorite historian, demanded that
Spain pay "a just and reasonable indemnity to the United States
for the heavy and necessary expenses which they have been compelled to incur by the failure of Spain to perform her engage-
ments to restrain the Indians."[25]

Tacitus's principle is understood by every petty crook who
knows enough to shout "Thief! Thief!" when caught with his
hands in someone's pocket. It is a standard propaganda ploy,
commonly adopted by powerful states to punish their victims:
France's demand that Haiti pay a huge indemnity to compensate
for its successful slave revolt is another famous example, with consequences that still endure, two centuries later. The technique is
also routine in mainstream media analysis. Adopting it, one can
overthrow mountains of evidence exposing media subservience
to state and private power by a flick of the wrist: simply ignore
the evidence, and ask whether the crusading media have gone too
far in their adversarial stance, perhaps even threatening the democratic process in their extreme anti-establishment bias.[26]

Nevertheless, in the history of state violence and intellectual
perfidy, it is doubtful that one can find an example of inversion
of guilt that compares with the case of the US wars in Indochina.

Anyone with a lingering belief that even a wisp of principle
or human concern might animate the ideological managers intent on arousing furor over the MIAs can readily overcome that
delusion by considering two crucial facts. The first is the complete lack of interest in the vastly greater number of MIAs from
earlier wars, whose remains are found accidentally to this day in
European battlegrounds and even Canada (from the US invasion

in 1812), areas where no one has ever hindered any search. The
second decisive fact is the history of the POW/MIA campaign.
It was carefully orchestrated to overcome rising public concern
about US atrocities that could no longer be suppressed—the Tacitus principle—and to derail negotiations that Nixon and
Kissinger sought to evade. After 1975, the issue was exploited as
a device to continue the war by other means.

The revival of the issue in the late 1980s was an entirely predictable consequence of Vietnam's withdrawal from Cambodia.
Its December 1979 invasion after murderous Khmer Rouge attacks on Vietnamese border areas, driving out Pol Pot and ter-
minating his atrocities, was portrayed by US leaders and political
commentators as a profound shock to their delicate sensibilities.
Naturally these apostles of Gandhi and Martin Luther King, so
devoted to international law, could react in only one way: by
helping to reconstitute the Khmer Rouge at the border, granting
the Pol Pot government diplomatic recognition, and insisting on
a central Khmer Rouge role in any settlement. To punish the perpetrators of this crime of aggression, they also had to maintain
the embargo that had been "bleeding Vietnam," as the *Far Eastern Economic Review* described the doctrine. When it was no
longer possible to deny that Vietnam had withdrawn its troops
from Cambodia in the context of the Paris Agreements, the cultural managers had to revert to the earlier pretext: the failure of
the Vietnamese to open their territory and archives to our inspec-
tion without impediment, and otherwise dedicate themselves to
the sole moral issue that remains unresolved from the war.

Meanwhile, respectable opinion is quite untroubled by the
study of the UN Transitional Authority in Cambodia (UNTAC),
unreported in the Free Press, which reveals that "there are indeed
foreign forces within the meaning of the Paris Agreements operating in Cambodia, but they are from Thailand," not Vietnam.
Army units of this long-time US dependency "move freely in the

DKZ [Democratic Kampuchea Zone, or Khmer Rouge-controlled territory] and have been accused of aiding the [Khmer Rouge] militarily," UNTAC reports, while aiding Thai businessmen active in gem and timber export in areas of Cambodia controlled by the Khmer Rouge, helping to finance Khmer Rouge operations while enriching themselves in good capitalist fashion.[27]

We might also add a third fact: the illegal and often brutal (even murderous) treatment by the US and Britain of Italian and German POWs during and after World War II, kept secret during the war for fear of German retaliation. This sorry record was exposed in the late 1970s, evoking much admiration in US commentary right at the time when fury about the perfidious Vietnamese was being whipped to a fever pitch. But we may drop these matters; though plainly relevant, they could not possibly enter mainstream discussion, or even be understood.[28]

The embargo imposed in 1975 "had the effect intended by Washington," *New York Times* correspondent Philip Shenon reports: "Malnutrition remains severe in northern and central Vietnam, and whatever the sudden wealth of many residents of Ho Chi Minh City, visitors to the city are often swarmed by families of homeless beggars," a vivid refutation of the claim that the US lost the war. "Vietnam's war-shattered economy has now only begun to recover" after 17 years in which the US "cut off not only the legal supply of American goods but also aid from the World Bank, the International Monetary Fund and other international lending agencies." "Most Vietnamese are dirt-poor now," the *Far Eastern Economic Review* reports, "but the economy is expected to boom once the embargo is dropped" and Vietnam can "become a low-wage platform for exporters of manufactured goods"—foreign investors, who can benefit from the US policy of first destroying and then bleeding Vietnam. The *Review* reports the concern of US firms that rivals from other countries may beat them out. "US companies have suffered irretrievable market-share losses in Vietnam," the director of a trade and investment company complains, as competitors have begun to break the US-imposed embargo. US firms want Washington to continue to "shut the door of international financial institutions to Vietnam" to prevent any recovery until the embargo is lifted, so that they can gain their proper share, recognizing, as the *Financial Times* reports, that "Funds from the World Bank, the International Monetary Fund and the Asian Development Bank, currently blocked by Washington, are urgently needed" if there is to be any substantial recovery—or profits.[29]

Blood-lust has its merits, but money talks even louder. The embargo has plainly outlived its usefulness.

"The Japanese do not hide their enthusiasm for the skills and dedication—and low wages—of Vietnamese workers," Victor Mallet reports in the *Financial Times.* They are preparing to invest to benefit from these useful consequences of the American war and postwar strangulation. But the Godfather has not lost his clout entirely: "the Japanese government and Japanese companies are still anxious not to offend the US by undertaking high-profile projects in Vietnam," Mallet reports, and are still "very, very cautious," a Mitsui representative adds. But they are moving forward slowly, frightening American firms.

"Through the 1980s, U.S. officials emphasized that Vietnam should end its occupation of Cambodia before the U.S. embargo could be lifted, "Robert Greenberger reports in the *Wall Street Journal:* "After Vietnam withdrew its troops, the U.S. then stressed the need to resolve the MIA and POW issues before relations could be restored," and now Washington "is under pressure from American companies to resolve the [MIA] issue so that they...[will not]...be left behind in the race for access to Vietnam's markets and resources, including potentially rich offshore oil deposits." No conclusion is drawn from this transparent charade.

Like a good and loyal trooper, Steven Holmes reports in the

New York Times that the Bush Administration is moving to ease the trade embargo in "response to what the Administration sees as greater Vietnamese cooperation in the search for American servicemen still missing from the Vietnam war." The headline reads: "Hanoi's Help With M.I.A.'s Leads to Easing of Embargo." True, "business and trade organizations have also been lobbying the Administration to loosen the embargo," fearing that "they will lose out to Japanese companies in the Vietnam market"; and they "believe that there is more money to be made in Vietnam in the next 10 years" than in China. But the doctrinal truths are unshaken: it is Vietnam's greater willingness to face up to its crimes against us that led Mr. Bush to ease the trade embargo, an act that "signals a clear warming toward Vietnam after decades of bitterness and distrust spawned by Hanoi's invasion of Cambodia, its unwillingness to be forthcoming about the fate of missing Americans and lingering resentment toward Vietnam for having defeated the United States"—the last, an interesting departure from ritual.

Though Administration officials "have praised Hanoi for meeting a number of the conditions set by the president last year," Pamela Constable reports, "to many Americans...none of these arguments carry enough weight to overcome the deep bitterness, mistrust and hostility that linger" towards "an adversary that has delayed, deceived, and resisted legitimate US demands on the missing servicemen for years." Eager to resume ties with the US, the Vietnamese Government "is careful not to offend American visitors by suggesting directly that the sacrifice of Vietnamese families was greater than that of families in the United States," Philip Shenon adds.[30]

The drama continued through 1992. A year after he celebrated JFK's aggression by extending the US embargo, President Bush announced, in properly statesmanlike terms, that "It was a bitter conflict, but Hanoi knows today that we seek only answers without the threat of retribution for the past." We can never forgive them for what they have done to us, but "we can begin writing the last chapter of the Vietnam war" if they turn from other pursuits to locating the remains of missing Americans. The adjacent front-page story reports the visit of the Japanese Emperor to China, where he failed to "unambiguously" accept the blame "for [Japan's] wartime aggression," revealing again the deep flaw in the Japanese character that so sorely puzzles American commentators.[31]

8. Stable Guidelines

The next two chapters are devoted to the record of planning for the Vietnam War in the crucial 1961-1964 period (chapter 1) and the reshaping of interpretations as conditions changed, a matter of much independent interest (chapter 2).

There are several sources of evidence to be considered: (1) The historical facts; (2) public statements; (3) the internal planning record; (4) the memoirs and other reports of Kennedy insiders. In each category, the material is substantial. The record of internal deliberations, in particular, has been available far beyond the norm since the release of two editions of the *Pentagon Papers*, and of other documents since. The recent publication of thousands of pages of documents in the official State Department history for 1961-1964 provides a wealth of additional material.[32] Military histories, particularly province studies, also give much insight into the events and what lay behind them.

While history never permits anything like definitive conclusions, in this case, the richness of the record, and its consistency, permit some unusually confident judgments, in my opinion. The basic story that emerges from the historical and documentary record seems to me, in brief, as follows.[33]

Policy towards Vietnam fell within the general framework of post-World War II global planning, and faced little challenge until the general framework was modified in the early 1970s, partly as a consequence of the Indochina Wars.[34] The US quickly threw in its lot with France, fully aware that it was opposing the nationalist forces and that its clients could not withstand political competition. For these reasons, resort to peaceful means was never an option; rather, a threat to be avoided. It was also understood that the wars and subversion had little support at home. The operation therefore had to be wound up without too much delay, leaving Indochina under the control of client regimes, to the extent feasible.

Basic policies held firm from 1950 into the early 1970s, though by the end questions of feasibility and cost became pressing. The Geneva agreements of 1954 were at once subverted. The US imposed a client regime in what came to be called "South Vietnam." Lacking popular support, the regime resorted to large-scale terror to control the population, finally eliciting resistance, which it could not control. As Kennedy took office, the US position seemed to face imminent collapse. Kennedy therefore escalated the war in 1961-1962. The military command was exuberant over the success of the enhanced violence, and thought that the war could soon be wound up, leading to a military victory and US withdrawal. Kennedy went along with these predictions with reservations, never fully willing to commit himself to the withdrawal proposals put forth by his advisers.

Without exception, withdrawal proposals were conditioned on military victory. Every known Administration plan was explicit on that score, notably the October 1963 "program to replace U.S. personnel with trained Vietnamese *without impairment of the war effort*," coupled with instructions from the President to "increase effectiveness of war effort" so as to ensure "our fundamental objective of victory" (my emphasis).

By mid-1963, coercive measures appeared to be successful in the countryside, but internal repression had evoked large-scale urban protest. Furthermore, the client regime was calling for a reduction of the US role or even US withdrawal, and was making overtures for a peaceful settlement with the North. Given its unwavering commitment to "our fundamental objective of victory," the Kennedy Administration therefore resolved to overthrow its client in favor of a military junta that would be fully committed to this objective. The planned coup took place on November 1, 1963, placing the Generals in control.

As the US command had predicted, the coup led to further disintegration, and as the bureaucratic structure of the former regime dissolved, to a belated recognition that reports of military progress were built on sand. Furthermore, the Generals also proved unwilling to accept the US objective; Vietnamese on all sides were seeking some kind of accommodation that would avert the devastating war that was becoming increasingly likely if the US persisted in its demand for military victory.[35]

After the November 1 coup, tactics were modified in light of two new factors: (1) the hope that at last a stable basis had been established for expanded military action, and (2) recognition that the military situation in the countryside was a shambles. The first factor made escalation possible, the second made it necessary, as the former hopes were seen to be a mirage. The plans to withdraw soon had to be abandoned as the precondition collapsed. As it became evident that US forces could not withdraw "without impairment of the war effort," the withdrawal plans explicitly based on this condition were nullified; subsequent events made it clear that US forces would in fact have to be *increased* to achieve the "fundamental objective of victory," which was transmitted unchanged to the Johnson Administration. By early 1965, only a large-scale US invasion could prevent a political settlement.

The policy assumptions, never seriously challenged, allowed few options: the attack against South Vietnam was sharply escalated in early 1965, and the war was extended to the North.

By 1967, the military command was again beginning to see "light at the end of the tunnel," and to propose withdrawal. These hopes were dashed by the January 1968 Tet Offensive, which revealed that the war could not be quickly won. By then, domestic protest and deterioration of the US economy vis-à-vis its industrial rivals convinced domestic elites that the US should move towards disengagement.

These decisions set in motion the withdrawal of US ground forces, combined with another sharp escalation of the military assault against South Vietnam, and by then all of Indochina, in the hope that the basic goals could still be salvaged. Negotiations continued to be deferred as long as possible, and when the US was finally compelled to sign a peace treaty in January 1973, Washington announced at once, in the clearest and most explicit terms, that it would subvert the agreement in every crucial respect. That it proceeded to do, in particular, by increasing the violence in the South in violation of the treaty, with much domestic acclaim as the tactic appeared to be successful. The dissident press could tell the story, but the mainstream was entirely closed to such heretical truths, and still is, a ban maintained with impressive rigor.[36] These actions of the US and its client again elicited a reaction, and the client regime again collapsed. This time the US could not rescue it. By 1975, the war ended.

As already discussed, the US achieved a partial victory, but no more than that. On the negative side, the client regimes had fallen. But there was a silver lining: Indochina was in ruins, there was no fear that the "virus" of successful development might "infect" others, and the region was insulated from any residual danger, by murderous military regimes. Another consequence, predictable years earlier, was that the indigenous forces in South Vietnam and Laos, unable to resist the US onslaught, had been decimated, leaving North Vietnam as the dominant force in Indochina.[37] As to what might have happened had these forces survived and the countries been allowed to develop in their own ways, one can only speculate. Servants of power are ready to offer required answers, but these are without interest, reflecting only doctrinal needs.

Basic policy remained constant in essentials: disentanglement from an unpopular and costly venture as soon as possible, but only after the virus was destroyed and victory assured (by the 1970s, with increasing doubt that US client regimes could be sustained). Tactics were modified with changing circumstances and perceptions. Changes of Administration, including the Kennedy assassination, had no large-scale effect on policy, and not even any great effect on tactics, when account is taken of the objective situation and how it was perceived.

This seems to me to be a good first approximation to the general picture. We turn to details for the 1961-1964 period directly.

9. The Kennedy Revival

The forgotten anniversary of JFK's aggression was marked by more than President Bush's renewal of the embargo against Vietnam and renewed indignation over Vietnam's savage maltreatment of innocent America. It was also the occasion for renewed fascination with the Kennedy era, even adulation for the fallen leader who had escalated the attack against Vietnam from terror to aggression just 30 years earlier. This curious coincidence was based upon the claim, prominently advanced, that Kennedy intended to withdraw from Vietnam; and was assassinated for that reason, some alleged. The revival was spurred by Oliver Stone's film *JFK*, which reached a mass audience at that time with its message that Kennedy was secretly planning to end the Vietnam War, a plan aborted by the assassination.

The admiration for the lonely hero struck down as (and perhaps because) he sought to prevent a US war in Vietnam, and more muted variants with their associated theses, add an interest-

ing touch to the questions that would have arisen in a civilized society on the 30th anniversary of Kennedy's war, and the 500th anniversary of the conquest of which it was a particularly ugly part.
Such thoughts aside, the factual issues raised are of considerable
interest, well beyond the specific matter of Indochina policy.

The Kennedy revival involves disparate groups. One consists
of leading intellectuals of the Kennedy circle. What is interesting
in this case is not their rising to Kennedy's defense, but the way
they seized upon the idea that Kennedy was planning to withdraw from Vietnam, the timing of this thesis, and the comparison
to the version of these events they had provided before the war
became unpopular among elites. Among this group, few if any
credit the belief that the alleged withdrawal plans, or other
planned policy reversals, were a factor in the assassination.

A second category includes segments of the popular movements that in large part grew from opposition to the Vietnam War.
Their attitudes toward the man who escalated the war from terror
to aggression are perhaps more surprising, though it should be
recalled that the picture of Kennedy as the leader who was about
to lead us to a bright future of peace and justice was carefully nur-
tured during the Camelot years, with no little success, and has
been regularly revived in the course of the critique of the Warren
report and the attempts to construct a different picture, which
have reached and influenced a wide audience over the years.

Within both categories, some have taken the position that
JFK truly departed from the political norm, and had become (or
always was) committed to far-reaching policy changes: not only
was he planning to withdraw from Vietnam (the core thesis), but
also to break up the CIA and the military-industrial complex, to
end the Cold War, and otherwise to pursue directions that would
indeed have been highly unpopular in the corridors of power.
Others reject these assessments, but argue that Kennedy was
perceived as a dangerous reformer by right-wing elements (which

is undoubtedly true, as it is true of virtually everyone in public life). At this point, the speculations interweave with questions and theories about the assassination. Some take the position that Kennedy was assassinated by a high-level conspiracy determined to make sure that their own man, the hawkish LBJ, would take the reins. It is then necessary to assume further that a conspiracy of quite a remarkable character has concealed the awesome crime. There are other variants.

Of all of these theories, the only ones of any general interest are those that assume a massive cover-up, and a high-level conspiracy that required that operation. In that case, the assassination was an event of true political significance, breaking sharply from the normal course of politics and exercise of power. Such ideas make little sense unless coupled with the thesis that JFK was undertaking radical policy changes, or perceived to be by policy insiders.

The scale of the presumed conspiracy should be appreciated. There is not a phrase in the voluminous internal record hinting at any thought of such a notion. It must be, then, that personal discipline was extraordinary among a huge number of people, or that the entire record has been scrupulously sanitized. There has not been a single leak over thirty years, though a high-level conspiracy to assassinate Kennedy and conceal the crime would have to involve not only much of the government and the media, but a good part of the historical, scientific, and medical professions. An achievement so immense would be utterly without precedent or even remote analogue.

The conviction that JFK was assassinated by a high-level conspiracy, and that the crime has since been concealed by a conspiracy awesome in scale, is widely held in the grassroots movements and among left intellectuals. Indeed, it is often presented as established truth, the starting point for further discussion.[38]

Across this broad spectrum, there is a shared belief that history changed course dramatically when Kennedy was assassinated in November 1963. Many believe that the event casts a shadow over all that followed, opening an era of political illegitimacy, with the country in the hands of dark forces.

Given the strong reactions that these issues have raised, perhaps it is worthwhile to make clear just what is and is not under consideration in what follows. This discussion addresses the question of the assassination only at the policy level: is there any reason to believe that JFK broke from the general pattern and intended to withdraw US forces from Vietnam even if that would lead to "impairment of the war effort" and undermine the "fundamental objective of victory"? Ancillary questions arise concerning the further beliefs about impending policy changes. These questions are addressed below.

The issue of the assassination is only obliquely touched by these considerations. They imply nothing about the thesis that JFK was killed by the mafia, or by right-wing Cubans, or other such theories. They bear only on the thesis that Kennedy was killed in a high-level conspiracy followed by a cover-up of remarkable dimensions. Serious proponents of such theses have recognized that credible direct evidence is lacking, and have therefore sought indirect evidence, typically holding that JFK's plans for withdrawal from Vietnam (or some of the broader policy claims) provide the motive for the cabal. If serious, the claim must be that the high-level conspirators knew something not publicly available, or had beliefs based on such material; hence the importance of the internal planning record for advocates of such theses. This line of argument has been at the core of the revival of the past few years. Currently available evidence indicates that it is entirely without foundation, indeed in conflict with substantial evidence. Advocates of the thesis will have to look elsewhere, so it appears.

The available facts, as usual, lead us to seek the institutional sources of policy decisions and their stability. Individuals and

personal whim doubtless make a difference; one might, for example, speculate that the notorious Kennedy macho streak
might have led to dangerous escalation in Indochina, or that he
might have leaned towards an enclave strategy of the type advocated by his close adviser General Maxwell Taylor, or a Nixonian
modification with intensified bombing and murderous "accelerated pacification" but many fewer US ground combat forces;
while at home, he might not have committed himself to "great
society" and civil rights issues to the extent LBJ did. Or one
might make other guesses. They are baseless, and hold little interest. In the present case, there is a rich record to assist us in
understanding the roots of policy and its implementation. People
who want to understand and change the world will do well, in
my opinion, to pay attention to it, not to engage in groundless
speculation as to what one or another leader might have done.

1

From Terror to Aggression

1. The Doctrinal Framework

To understand Kennedy's war and the aftermath it is necessary to attend to the thinking that lay behind the policy choices. Kennedy planners adopted doctrines already established. Too much independence ("radical nationalism") is not acceptable; the "rotten apple" effect of possible success enhances the need to eliminate the "infection" before it spreads. The Indochina wars are only a special case, which happened to get out of hand. In this general context, independent nationalism was unthinkable, and was never seriously entertained as an option.

By 1948 Washington planners recognized that the nationalist movement was led by Ho Chi Minh and the Viet Minh. Ho was eager to cooperate with the United States, but not on the required terms of subordination. Furthermore, top policymakers feared, Vietnamese independence might fan "anti-Western Pan-Asiatic tendencies in the region," undermining the "close association between newly-autonomous peoples and powers which have been long responsible [for] their welfare"; in Indochina, the responsible authority was France, whose tender care had left the countries devastated and starving. Chinese influence, in contrast, must be excluded "so that the peoples of Indochina will not be hampered in their natural developments

49

by the pressure of an alien people and alien interests"; unlike the US and France.

The US right to restore the "close association" is axiomatic. It follows that any problems that arise can be attributed to illegitimate nationalist aspirations. On these assumptions, the CIA warned in September 1948 that "The gravest danger to the US is that friction engendered by [anticolonialism and economic nationalism] may drive the so-called colonial bloc into alignment with the USSR": Third World nationalism is the cause of the "friction," not imperial concerns. The traditional "colonial economic interests" of the industrial countries must prevail if "friction" interferes with US global plans. Southeast Asia would have to remain under "its traditional subordination," Melvyn Leffler observes, reviewing a broad scholarly consensus.[1]

The major concern was Japan, the "superdomino" (John Dower). Internally, the old order had to be restored and Japan protected from what the State Department called the "concealed aggression" of the Russians, referring to internal political developments that might threaten business rule. And Japan had to be deterred from independent foreign and economic policies, from "the suicide of neutralism" (General Omar Bradley) and accommodation to China. The only hope for achieving these goals, George Kennan argued, lay in restoring for Japan "some sort of Empire toward the South." In effect, the US must provide Japan with its wartime "co-prosperity sphere," now safely within the US-dominated world system, with no fear that US business interests would be denied their proper place.[2]

The guiding concerns are articulated in the public record as well. Outlining the "falling dominoes" theory in a news conference on April 7, 1954, President Eisenhower warned that Japan would have to turn "toward the Communist areas in order to live" if Communist success in Indochina "takes away, in its economic aspects, that region that Japan must have as a trading area." The consequences would be "just incalculable to the free world." Walter LaFeber observed in 1968 that "This thesis became a controlling assumption: the loss of Vietnam would mean the economic undermining and probable loss of Japan to Communist markets and ultimately to Communist influence if not control." Eisenhower's public statements expressed the conclusion of NSC 5405 (January 16) that "the loss of Southeast Asia, especially of Malaya and Indonesia, could result in such economic and political pressures in Japan as to make it extremely difficult to prevent Japan's eventual accommodation to communism." Communist domination of Southeast Asia "by whatever means" would "critically endanger" US "security interests," understood in the usual sense. The "loss of Vietnam" would therefore be of great significance; that it is ours to "lose" is again axiomatic.[3]

Given such doctrines, it is clear why the diplomatic settlement at the1954 Geneva conference was regarded as a disaster. Washington reacted vigorously. A few days after the accords were signed, the National Security Council decreed that even in the case of "local Communist subversion or rebellion *not constituting armed attack,*" the US would consider the use of military force, including an attack on China if it is "determined to be the source" of the "subversion" (NSC 5429/2; my emphasis).

This wording, repeated verbatim annually through the 1950s in planning documents, was chosen so as to make explicit the US right to violate the basic principles of the UN Charter, which bar any threat or use of force except in resistance to "armed attack" (until the UN Security Council acts). The same document called for remilitarizing Japan, converting Thailand into "the focal point of U.S. covert and psychological operations in Southeast Asia," undertaking "covert operations on a large and effective scale" throughout Indochina, and in every possible way undermining the Geneva accords.

This critically important document is grossly falsified by the
Pentagon Papers historians, and has largely disappeared from
history.[4]

Recall that "subversion," like "concealed aggression," is a
technical concept covering any form of unwelcome internal political development. Thus the Joint Chiefs, in 1955, outline "three
basic forms of aggression": armed attack across a border (aggression in the literal sense); "Overt armed attack from within the
area of each of the sovereign states"; "Aggression other than
armed, i.e., political warfare, or subversion." An internal uprising
against a US-imposed police state, or elections that come out the
wrong way, are forms of "aggression," which the US has the right
to combat by arbitrary violence. The assumptions are so ingrained
as to pass without notice, as when liberal hero Adlai Stevenson,
UN Ambassador under Kennedy and Johnson, declared that in
Vietnam the US is defending a free people from "internal aggression." Stevenson compared this noble cause to the first major
postwar counterinsurgency campaign, in Greece in 1947, where
US-run operations successfully demolished the anti-Nazi resistance and the political system and restored the old order, including
leading Nazi collaborators, at the cost of some 160,000 lives and
tens of thousands of victims of torture chambers, and a legacy of
destruction yet to be overcome (along with great benefits to US
corporations). Similar premises are adopted routinely by apolo-
gists for state violence; thus Sidney Hook condemned the "incur-
sions" of the indigenous South Vietnamese resistance, praising
the US for using armed might to counter these crimes despite
the "unfortunate accidental loss of life" in such exercises as satu-
ration bombing by B-52s in the densely-populated Delta.[5]

The character of the intellectual culture is indicated by the
reaction to such thoughts.

In accordance with the plans laid out in NSC 5429/2, Washington moved at once to subvert the Geneva settlement, in-

stalling a client regime in the South: the GVN (RVN), which regarded itself throughout as the legitimate government of all Vietnam. With US backing and guidance, the GVN launched a massive terrorist attack against the domestic population and barred the planned 1956 elections on unification, which were the condition under which the resistance had accepted the Geneva accords. The subversion was recognized to be successful: as Kennedy's chief war manager Robert McNamara observed while once again rejecting diplomatic options in March 1964, "Only the U.S. presence after 1954 held the South together under far more favorable circumstances, and enabled Diem to refuse to go through with the 1954 provision calling for nationwide 'free' elections in 1956."[6]

The facts are described with fair accuracy by US military intelligence. A 1964 study observes that after the Geneva agreements of 1954 that "partitioned" Vietnam, the DRV (North Vietnam) relocated 100,000 people to the North, including 40,000 military personnel, leaving behind "Several thousand political agitators and activists" and some military forces "with orders to remain dormant." "In 1956, the US-backed president of the RVN—Ngo Dinh Diem—blocked the referendum called for by the Geneva Agreements which was to decide the form of government that would rule over a reunited Vietnam. The Communists, who saw their hopes for a legal takeover of the whole country vanish by this maneuver, ordered their dormant 'stay behinds' to commence propaganda activities to put pressure on the new and inexperienced government of the RVN," perhaps hoping "to overthrow the government without having to resort to military activity." By 1957, they "instituted a program of proselytizing RVN armed forces officers and men to the VC cause," also following "the standard Communist tactic of infiltrating and subverting legal political parties." In 1958-1959, "having achieved a degree of popular support in the rural areas through pressure, argument, terror and subversion," the VC began to organize guerrilla groups among the local populace, later supported by southerners returning from the North (all military infiltrators being "veterans of the French Indo-China War who had served in the area now governed by the RVN" through 1963, this MACV [Military Assistance Command, Vietnam] Intelligence Infiltration Study reports).[7]

It is only necessary to add a few minor corrections. The Geneva agreements did not "partition" Vietnam but separated two military zones by a temporary demarcation line that "should not in any way be interpreted as constituting a political or territorial boundary," pending the unification elections of 1956 that were the heart of the accords. Intelligence is adopting "the standard US tactic" of denouncing political action that is out of control as subversion. The US client regime was carrying out wholesale terror to block such "subversion" and destroy the anti-French resistance, finally compelling the latter to resort to violence in self-defense. JFK raised the level of the US attack from international terrorism to outright aggression in 1961-1962. Apart from Americans, the only non-South Vietnamese forces in South Vietnam were US mercenaries, primarily South Korean and Chinese. That aside, US intelligence has the story more or less straight.

Well after regular US bombing of North Vietnam began in February 1965, North Vietnamese units were detected in border areas or across the border, though Korean mercenaries alone far outnumbered North Vietnamese as of March 1966 and matched their numbers until the Tet Offensive (also, incidentally, providing 20 percent of South Korea's foreign currency revenue and thus helping to spark the later economic miracle). There were also Chinese forces, namely mercenaries from Chiang Kai-Shek's army introduced by Kennedy and Johnson, six companies of combat infantry by April 1965. North Vietnamese regular units, estimated by the Pentagon at about 50,000 by 1968, were largely in peripheral areas; US mercenary forces, in contrast, were rampaging in the heartland, as was the US military itself. Korean mercenaries, who were particularly brutal, reached 50,000 by 1969, along with another 20,000 "Free World" and over a half-million US troops.[8]

Washington's principled opposition to political settlement continued without change. From the early 1960s, there was intense concern over French President Charles de Gaulle's proposals for neutralization, as well as initiatives towards a peaceful resolution of the conflict by Vietnamese on all sides, including the Diem regime and the Generals who replaced it. A political settlement might have extended as far as neutralization of Laos, Cambodia, and South Vietnam, as advocated by the National Liberation Front (the "Viet Cong" of US propaganda). As discussed above, the US was adamantly opposed to any such possibility. Fear of neutralization was one factor in the Kennedy-inspired coup that overthrew Diem, and considerable pressures were exerted to bring de Gaulle to retract his initiatives, which appeared still more threatening in the context of Kennedy's concerns about his role in promoting the "suicide of neutralism" in Europe.

France's position on Vietnam was explained by Foreign Minister Couve de Murville, in response to a request (April 1964) to clarify what France meant by the term "neutrality." Couve's reply was: "Quite simply, the Geneva Agreements of 1954," which he interpreted as meaning "the division of Viet-Nam with a commitment by both sides not to accept military aid from outside (sic) and not to enter into military alliances—which is really neutrality." "The South Vietnamese people are out of the game," Couve added. "All you have is a professional army supported from outside."[9]

The Kennedy and Johnson Administrations knew very well that the generals are "all we have got" and that "We are at present

overwhelmingly outclassed politically" (Ambassador Henry
Cabot Lodge, January 1964). That is precisely why Washington
always regarded diplomacy as anathema: lacking political support, the US could put forth no credible negotiating position. So
the story continues right through to the end.[10]

The basic reasoning about diplomacy is stated clearly in the
internal record. As the US position was collapsing in 1964 and
calls were mounting for an attack against the North, William
Bundy wrote that diplomacy could be considered "After, *but only
after,* we have established a clear pattern of pressure hurting the
DRV and leaving no doubts in South Vietnam of our resolve" (his
emphasis). First force, then diplomacy—a last resort, if we are
sure that we are powerful enough to win.[11]

For similar reasons, opposition to negotiations and diplomacy has been a characteristic US policy stance in Latin America
and the Middle East, and remains so, as documented in extensive detail elsewhere. Commentators assume as a matter of
course that diplomacy is a threat to be avoided. The principle is
considered uncontroversial, a truism, perhaps even more so than
in the past. In January 1993, when the West alleged that Iraq was
moving missiles within its territory contrary to US wishes (but
in accord with UN resolutions), the United States demanded
that they be removed. In response, Iraq called for negotiations
on all disputed issues, "An exchange that recalls the maneuvering
before the gulf war," the *New York Times* reported, highlighting
these words. "The ultimatum and Iraq's reply today recalled the
maneuvering before the Persian Gulf War, in which the allies set
a firm deadline for Iraqi compliance while Baghdad sought un-
successfully to fend off military action with diplomatic tactics,"
the front-page story reported. Pursuit of peaceful means as required by international law and the UN Charter is a crime that
Washington must resolutely resist, keeping to the weapon of violence, in which it reigns supreme; that is unquestioned dogma.

It is natural that those who are militarily strong but politically weak will prefer the arena of violence. Apparent exceptions typically reflect the failure of force or perceived advantage. The solemn obligation to pursue peaceful means is notable by its absence in affairs of state. It is part of the responsibility of the cultural managers in every society to cloak such facts in pieties about the high ideals and nobility of leaders, and to reshape the facts for public consumption.[12]

States are not moral agents; those who attribute to them ideals and principles merely mislead themselves and others.

Public rhetoric reflecting the guiding policy doctrines sometimes rose to near-hysteria. In June 1956, Senator John F. Kennedy stated that:

> Vietnam represents the cornerstone of the Free World in Southeast Asia, the Keystone to the arch, the finger in the dike. Burma, Thailand, India, Japan, the Philippines and, obviously, Laos and Cambodia are among those whose security would be threatened if the red tide of Communism overflowed into Vietnam... Moreover, the independence of Free Vietnam is crucial to the free world in fields other than the military. Her economy is essential to the economy of all of Southeast Asia; and her political liberty is an inspiration to those seeking to obtain or maintain their liberty in all parts of Asia—and indeed the world. The fundamental tenets of this nation's foreign policy, in short, depend in considerable measure upon a strong and free Vietnamese nation

—which was then enjoying its "inspiring political liberty" under the Diem dictatorship, a Latin American-style terror state dedicated to the murder and torture of people committed to the Geneva settlement and other forms of "concealed aggression."[13]

Kennedy kept to these extremist doctrines. As he prepared to escalate the war to direct US aggression in late 1961, he warned that "we are opposed around the world by a monolithic and ruthless conspiracy that relies primarily on covert means for expanding its sphere of influence"; if the conspiracy achieves its ends in Laos and Vietnam, "the gates will be opened wide." "The complacent, the self-indulgent, the soft societies are about to be swept away with the debris of history [and] Only the strong...can possibly survive," Kennedy railed, outraged in this case by Cuba's unconscionable defeat of the Bay of Pigs invasion. Until the end he held that we must support the GVN in its "struggle to maintain its national independence"; "for us to withdraw from that effort would mean a collapse not only of South Viet-Nam, but Southeast Asia. So we are going to stay there" (July 17, 1963). "I don't agree with those who say we should withdraw," he said in a September 2 TV interview with Walter Cronkite: "That would be a great mistake... It doesn't do us any good to say, 'Well, why don't we all just go home and leave the world to those who are our enemies'... We are going to meet our responsibility." In an NBC interview a week later (September 9), Kennedy rejected withdrawal outright: "I think we should stay," he said. We should not withdraw because withdrawal "only makes it easy for the Communists," who would sweep over Southeast Asia. Three days later he made his position still clearer:

> What helps to win the war, we support; what interferes with the war effort, we oppose. I have already made it clear that any action by either government which may handicap the winning of the war is inconsistent with our policy or our objectives. This is the test which I think every agency and official of the United States Government must apply to all of our actions...But we have a very simple policy in that area...: we want the war to be won, the Communists to be contained, and the Americans to go home...But we are not there to see a war lost, and we will follow the policy which I have indicated today of advancing those causes and issues which help win the war.

These September 12 remarks became "a policy guideline," Roger Hilsman noted in 1967. Hilsman cited them as such in a plan for Vietnam that he and his associates prepared, at the President's request, and sent to JFK on September 16 (see below).

On September 26, Kennedy amplified further. We keep troops in Vietnam and elsewhere, he said, because "our freedom is tied up with theirs" and the "security of the United States is thereby endangered" if they pass "behind the Iron Curtain." "So all those who suggest we withdraw [in any way], I could not disagree with them more." "If the United States were to falter, the whole world, in my opinion, would inevitably begin to move toward the Communist bloc."[14]

Aid reductions are excluded, Kennedy stated on March 6, 1963, because tampering with "economic programs and military programs in South Viet-Nam, in Cambodia, in Thailand" would cause "that area to collapse," leading to Communist control of "all of Southeast Asia, with the inevitable effect" of threatening India and perhaps even the Middle East. There is, then, no "real prospect of the burden being lightened for the U.S. in Southeast Asia in the next year if we are going to do the job and meet what I think are very clear national needs." It is our "objective" to ensure that "the assault from the inside, and which is manipulated from the North, is ended" (November 12, 1963). The natural conclusion is that we must go to the source and punish the manipulators if we fail to contain the "assault from the inside" by South Vietnamese peasants against US forces and their agents.

After the Diem regime was overthrown on November 1, 1963, there was a "new situation there," Kennedy told the press, and "we hope, an increased effort in the war" (November 14). He added that our policy should now be to "intensify the struggle" so that "we can bring Americans out of there"—after victory, as the context makes unmistakably clear.

In Fort Worth, a few hours before the assassination, Kennedy made his last statement about Vietnam: "Without the United States, South Vietnam would collapse overnight." In the speech he was to give in Dallas, he intended to say that "Our successful defense of freedom" in Cuba, Laos, the Congo, and Berlin can be attributed "not to the words we used, but to the strength we stood ready to use"; fair enough, with regard to his selection of Third World illustrations of his "defense of freedom." Kennedy extolled his huge military buildup, undertaken to blunt the "ambitions of international Communism." As the "watchman on the walls of world freedom" the US had to undertake tasks that were "painful, risky and costly, as is true in Southeast Asia today. But we dare not weary of the task."[15]

In internal discussion, Kennedy's consistent position was that everyone must "focus on winning the war." There can be no withdrawal without victory; the stakes are far too high. One can accuse the President of no duplicity. His public rhetoric accords closely with his stand in internal discussion.

Kennedy's closest associates maintained the same stance after the assassination. "Unless we can achieve [our] objective in South Vietnam," Robert McNamara informed LBJ in a March 1964 memorandum, "almost all of Southeast Asia will probably fall under Communist dominance," with threats going beyond Burma, Malaysia, Indonesia, and Thailand to the Philippines, India, Australia and New Zealand, Taiwan, Korea, and Japan. "The stakes are high." In a note to LBJ on June 11, Robert Kennedy expressed his full support, saying that Vietnam "is obviously the most important problem facing the United States and if you felt I could help I am at your service." As a token of his support, he expressed his willingness to replace Lodge as Ambassador to Saigon. In May 1965, three months after the bombing of South Vietnam had been vastly intensified along with the first regular bombing of the North and after US combat forces had landed, RFK condemned withdrawal as "a repudiation of commitments undertaken and confirmed by three administrations" which would "gravely—perhaps irreparably—weaken the democratic position in Asia." Theodore Sorenson traces RFK's first break with Johnson policy to February 1966, when RFK called for a negotiated settlement (but not withdrawal, never an option).[16]

The basic reasoning behind the war was indicated years later by McGeorge Bundy. In retrospect, he felt that "our effort" in

Vietnam was "excessive" after October 1965, when "a new anti-communist government took power in Indonesia and destroyed the communist party," incidentally, slaughtering several hundred thousand peasants and securing Indonesia's riches for foreign corporations. As Bundy now recognized, with Vietnam already in ruins and Indonesia protected against infection, it may have been "excessive" to continue to demolish Indochina at inordinate cost to ourselves. US-supported military coups in Thailand and the Philippines, the virtual demolition of most of Indochina, and the subsequent policies of economic strangulation and isolation brought the US at least a partial victory, ensuring that the region will continue to "fulfill its main function," free from any threat of "radical nationalism." That the US won a considerable victory was clear to the international business community and others 20 years ago, as already discussed, though not by the standards of those who regard anything less than attainment of maximal aims as an unthinkable disaster. The questions therefore remain largely foreign to the intellectual culture.[17]

As the costs to the US began to mount, qualifications began to enter, and when disaster loomed, some proponents of "the domino theory" backed away or even derided it. But Kennedy and his circle did not waver in their extremism as long as success seemed within reach. The same was true of intellectual opinion. McGeorge Bundy scarcely exaggerated when he wrote that only "wild men in the wings" questioned the basic assumptions of the Kennedy-Johnson war, raising more than tactical questions about feasibility and cost. Furthermore, that judgment remains largely valid today, in elite sectors.

2. Kennedy's War

Lacking popular support, the client government established by Eisenhower turned to extensive terror directed against the anti-French resistance (Viet Minh, later relabelled "Viet Cong"). "There

can be no doubt," a 1972 study prepared for the Pentagon concludes, "that innumerable crimes and absolutely senseless acts of
suppression against both real and suspected Communists and sym-
pathizing villagers were committed. Efficiency took the form of
brutality and a total disregard for the difference between determined foes and potential friends." Killing and repression began at
once, with over 10,000 killed by 1957. Bernard Fall estimates
about 66,000 killed between 1957 and 1961, another 89,000 between 1961 and April 1965, virtually all of them South Vietnamese,
victims of state terror or "the crushing weight of American armor,
napalm, jet bombers and finally vomiting gases."[18]

By 1956, military historian Eric Bergerud observes, "Many
of the most vulnerable cadres had already been imprisoned or
killed." Though Diem's post-Geneva terror "left the [Commu-
nist] Party reeling," through 1959 "the Party adhered to the policy of political rather than violent resistance" and "by and large
honored the Geneva Accords," having "dismantled the bulk of
its military apparatus," leaving its cadres "relatively disarmed." It
finally decided "to answer in kind" though with "a small-scale and
secret effort" until 1960, reaction that elicited hysterical outrage
in the United States over Communist perfidy.

Having lost its only asset, the monopoly of violence, the
GVN faced imminent collapse. As Kennedy took over, the US
position seemed desperate in both Laos and Vietnam. By 1961,
the *Pentagon Papers* report,

> it had become clear in both Saigon and Washington that the yellow star
> of the Viet Cong was in the ascendancy... The VC continued to hold
> the initiative in the countryside, controlling major portions of the pop-
> ulace and drawing an increasingly tight cinch around Saigon. The op-
> erative question was not whether the Diem government as it was then
> moving could defeat the insurgents, but whether it could save itself.

Kennedy accepted a diplomatic settlement, at least on paper, in
Laos, but chose to respond by military escalation in Vietnam.[19]

Under Eisenhower, the *Pentagon Papers* report, US forces
had been "strictly advisory," following the norm of the Latin
American terror states. But as JFK took over in 1961, "the U.S.
had in addition provided military capabilities such as helicopters
and tactical air support" by January 1962, following Kennedy's
authorization of USAF Farmgate operations in October. On November 22, 1961, the President authorized use of US forces "in
a sharply increased effort to avoid a further deterioration of the
situation in SVN [South Vietnam]," including "increased airlift
to the GVN in the form of helicopters, light aviation and trans-
port aircraft," and both equipment and US personnel "for aerial
reconnaissance, instruction in and execution of air-ground support and special intelligence." Included in the "US military units"
were three army Helicopter Companies, a Troop Carrier
Squadron with 32 planes, combat aircraft, a Reconnaissance
Unit, and six C-123 aircraft equipped for defoliation. On November 11, the NSC had authorized dispatch of "Aircraft, personnel and chemical defoliants to kill Viet Cong food crops and
defoliate selected border and jungle areas," and by November 27
it was reported that "spraying equipment had been installed on
Vietnamese H-34 helicopters, and is ready for use against food
crops." US military personnel were increased from 841 to 5,576
by June 30, 1962. MAAG [Military Assistance Advisory Group]
teams were extended to battalion level and were "beginning to
participate more directly in advising Vietnamese unit commanders in the planning and execution of military operations plans."
By February 1962, the US Air Force "had already flown hundreds of missions," John Newman writes, citing an army history,
often with only a low-ranking Vietnamese enlisted man for show.
In one week of May 1962, Vietnamese Air Force and US helicopter units flew about 350 sorties (offensive, airlift, etc.).[20]

US escalation led to "a noticeable improvement," Hilsman
wrote. In particular, "the helicopters were grand... Roaring in

over the treetops, they were a terrifying sight to the superstitious Viet Cong peasants," who "simply turned and ran," becoming "easy targets." Kennedy also authorized the use of napalm, which particularly delighted MACV Commander General Paul Harkins; asked about the consequences of napalming villages, he replied that it "really puts the fear of God into the Viet Cong." By mid-1962, the CIA was conducting intelligence and sabotage operations against the North, as well as "counter-terror" (the technical term for "our terror") in the South. The intent of Kennedy's 1961-1962 escalation was "to fight the insurgency by destroying its economic base and disrupting the social fabric of the areas where the Front was strongest" by a variety of means, later extended to "defoliation, air attack, and indiscriminate artillery bombardment of what later were to be called 'free fire zones'"(Bergerud).[21]

As military operations were intensified in 1962, the US military became concerned that "supporting air and artillery were an inducement [to ARVN, the GVN army] to rely on indiscriminate firepower as a substitute for aggressiveness." It was not long before State Department intelligence transmitted reports "that indiscriminate bombing in the countryside is forcing innocent or wavering peasants toward the Viet Cong" and that over 100,000 Montagnards had fled VC-controlled areas, in part because of "The extensive use of artillery and aerial bombardment and other apparently excessive and indiscriminate measures by GVN military and security forces," which have "undoubtedly killed many innocent peasants and made many others more willing than before to cooperate with the Viet Cong." Extensive use of air power and crop destruction might provoke "militant opposition among the peasants and positive identification with the Viet Cong," who were recruiting locally and depended on the local population for concealment and support (December 1962). Superhawk Dennis Duncanson of the British Advisory Mission reported that the policy of random bombardment of villages in "open zones" (where no restrictions applied) was the "principal cause of a huge migration of tribesmen in the summer of 1962," citing estimates from 125,000 to 300,000.

The problem caused by "increased aggressiveness," including use of artillery and air power "to 'soften up' the enemy" concealed among the population, was noted by Kennedy's dovish advisers Hilsman and National Security Staff member Michael Forrestal, who observed that "No one really knows...how many of the 20,000 'Viet Cong' killed last year [1962] were only innocent or at least persuadable villagers" and "it is impossible to assess how much resentment among persuadable villagers is engendered by the inevitable accidents" (attacks on the wrong village, for example). The same problems arose later in Laos, and in Cambodia, where total air war against the peasant community played a significant role in mobilizing the Khmer Rouge, as attested by US government studies and independent scholarship.[22]

By 1962, Kennedy's war had far surpassed the French war at its peak in helicopters and aerial fire power. As for personnel, France had 20,000 nationals fighting in all of Indochina in 1949 (US force levels reached 16,700 under JFK), increasing to 57,000 at the peak.[23]

Kennedy's aggression was no secret. In March 1962, US officials announced publicly that US pilots were engaged in combat missions (bombing and strafing). By October, after three US planes were shot down in two days, a front-page story in the *New York Times* reported that "in 30 percent of all the combat missions flown in Vietnamese Air Force planes, Americans are at the controls," though "national insignia have been erased from many aircraft, both American and Vietnamese, ...to avoid the thorny international problems involved." The press reported further that US Army fliers and gunners were taking the military initiative against southern guerrillas, using HU-1A helicopters, which had more firepower than any World War II fighter plane, as an offensive weapon. Armed helicopters were regularly supporting ARVN operations. US operations in 1962 in the Delta region in the southern sector of South Vietnam were reported by journalist Robert Shaplen, among others. [24]

The character of Kennedy's war was also no secret. In a 1963 book, journalist Richard Tregaskis reported his interviews with US helicopter pilots who described how "wild men" of the helicopter units would shoot civilians for sport in "solid VC areas." Describing visits to hamlets that had been hit by napalm and heavy bombs in US air strikes, Malcolm Browne, AP correspondent from 1961, observed that "there is no question that the results are revolting. Unfortunately, the Viet Cong builds bunkers so skillfully it is rarely touched by aerial bombs or napalm, except in cases of direct hits. But huts are flattened, and civilian loss of life is generally high. In some, the charred bodies of children and babies have made pathetic piles in the middle of the remains of market places."[25]

The character of Kennedy's war was revealed further by Roger Hilsman. In his 1967 book, he cites a December 19, 1962 report of his Bureau of Intelligence and Research, which identifies several problems. One is that "excessive use of air strikes in the absence of ground contact with the enemy continues to kill a lot of innocent peasants." Another is that the core element of the pacification program—the plan to drive some 7 million peasants into "strategic hamlets"—was not being well implemented. "The purpose of these measures is to isolate and protect the peasants from the Communists," but "excessive use of air power and crop destruction" and other terror techniques "may well develop a militant opposition from the peasants and their positive identification with the Viet Cong."

In retrospect, Hilsman also expressed his unhappiness about defoliation, which "was just too reminiscent of gas warfare," and napalm, "a standard item of issue" with "ample stockpiles"; the battle over its use "had long since been lost" by mid-1962. "What was debatable," he wrote in 1967, "was whether it was on balance a gain or a loss to bomb huts, 'structures,' and villages that had been reported to be Viet Cong." It was debatable for two reasons: first, intelligence was faulty so that the wrong villages might be struck; second, "indiscriminate bombing, or even carelessness in bombing, would turn the people toward the Viet Cong." It is these reservations that identify Hilsman as a leading dove.

To illustrate some of the problems, Hilsman described an operation of January 21, 1962. The senior American adviser who planned the operation called for an early morning attack by B-26s from the Farmgate squadron, who were to bomb and strafe a cluster of huts near the Cambodian border; "but through a tragic error in map-reading," Hilsman writes, "they in fact attacked a Cambodian village just over the border, killing and wounding a number of villagers." Fortunately, the error was quickly rectified. Five minutes later, the US bombers attacked the intended village with 500-pound bombs, along with T-28 rocket attacks. The huts were bombed and strafed for 45 minutes, wounding 11 civilians and killing 5 others, including children of 2, 5, and 7. An airborne battalion was then dropped by parachute. "Except for the error that led to bombing the Cambodian village, the plan was well and efficiently executed—but it was more appropriate to the European fronts of World War II than it was to guerrilla warfare." "The greatest problem," Hilsman continued, "is that bombing huts and villages will kill civilians and push the population still further toward active support for the Viet Cong"; that they did commonly support the Viet Cong, and that the GVN could only control them by force, was no secret to the head of State Department intelligence.

Hilsman favored counterinsurgency over World War II-style operations. He therefore supported British adviser Sir Robert Thompson's concept of strategic hamlets, into which South

Vietnamese were to be herded by force or random bombardment. These concentration camps, Hilsman explains, were to
"create the physical security the villager must have before he
could make a free choice between the Vietcong and the government," a "free choice" denied him in his native village. But the
plan failed. Citing Thompson, Hilsman notes that "there had
been no real effort to isolate the population from the Viet Cong
by eliminating Viet Cong agents and supporters inside the strategic hamlets and by imposing controls on the movement of people
and supplies." "Vietcong agents remained in place" and "some
Viet Cong supporters and agents...had no difficulty repenetrating
the hamlet and continuing subversion." The correct strategy
would have been to ensure that all such supporters and agents
were "eliminated before the troops and civic action teams moved
on to the next" area. "It seemed obvious that putting defenses
around a village would do no good if the defenses enclosed Viet
Cong agents," still free to talk to their brothers or cousins. "Free
choice" is available only under armed guard by an occupying
army in an encampment surrounded by barbed wire, with the
political opposition "eliminated." The *Pentagon Papers* analyst
adds that it was not easy to gain the loyalty of people who had
to be "herded forcibly from their homes," or bombed out of
them, and who, for some reason, showed "resentment if not active resistance" to these forthcoming efforts to offer them a "free
choice," American-style.[26]

Hilsman's views mark the dovish end of the Camelot spectrum. At the other extreme, Walt Rostow, General Curtis LeMay,
and others called for US force to get on with the job.

In his moral-historical tract, Guenter Lewy, who departs
from the official Party Line only in that he recognizes no category of "innocent peasants," reports that by the end of 1962, the
US had deployed 149 helicopters and 73 fixed-wing aircraft,
which had carried out 2,048 attack sorties. "Areas which could

not be penetrated by government forces were declared 'open zones,' and villages in them were subjected to random bombardment by artillery and aircraft so as to drive the inhabitants into the safety of the strategic hamlets," the idea being "to concentrate the rural population in fortified villages so as to provide them with physical security against the VC," who most supported, according to US government studies. The only problem is that "these measures of coercion further alienated the population," and were therefore unwise. The *Wehrmacht* officers who helped write the counterinsurgency manuals doubtless appreciated his sentiments.

Noted humanitarians took much the same position, for example, Leo Cherne, chairman of the executive committee of Freedom House and of the board of directors of the International Rescue Committee. This respected advocate of the rights of (certain) refugees wrote in December 1965 that "There are more than 700,000 additional refugees who have recently fled the countryside dominated by the Vietcong and with their act of flight have chosen the meager sanctuary provided by the government of South Vietnam." As he wrote, a US government-sponsored study observed that US air and artillery bombardment impel the villagers "to move where they will be safe from such attacks...regardless of their attitude to the GVN," facts hardly obscure to any person of minimal literacy at the time.[27]

And well before. It is worth noting that the US attack on South Vietnam, and the mounting atrocities, aroused no detectable interest or concern, just as the US-run terror campaign of the 1950s had passed with scarcely a raised eyebrow. And the more humane ideas of Hilsman and other doves, who preferred concentration camps and extermination of the political opposition to indiscriminate bombardment, were highly praised, criticized only for the incompetence of these efforts to provide a "free choice" to the South Vietnamese peasants we "protected." One of the more striking revelations in the *Pentagon Papers* was the utterly casual attitude towards terror and slaughter in the South, questioned only because of problems it might cause us among the targeted population and the embarrassment if B-52 raids "do not show significant results," which might make us "look silly and arouse criticism" (William Bundy). The decisions to bomb the North and to send US combat troops receive extensive deliberation. Virtually no attention is given to what Bernard Fall recognized at once as the fundamental policy decision of early 1965: "what changed the character of the Vietnam war," he wrote, "was *not* the decision to bomb North Vietnam; *not* the decision to use American ground troops in South Vietnam; but the decision to wage unlimited aerial warfare inside the country at the price of literally pounding the place to bits." In general, the population of the South was considered fair game for whatever the US chose to do.

This understanding was largely shared in the intellectual culture at home. The bombing of the North and the dispatch of US combat forces were controversial. Bombing of the South and other atrocities were not, until much later. The astonishing disparity of planning revealed in the *Pentagon Papers* also passed without notice, presumably being taken as obvious.[28]

The reasons are clear. The bombing of the North and the dispatch of US combat troops might be harmful to us. Slaughter in the South could be conducted with complete impunity, at least until popular opposition finally began to take shape. A comparison to Reagan's wars in Central America in the 1980s gives a useful measure of the cultural change brought about by the popular movements that finally arose, and explains why they have evoked such horror in many circles.

3. Shared Ground

It is well to be aware of just how much agreement there is about the nature of the war in the specialist literature. The consensus is well illustrated by the detailed and informative province studies. The first of these, and to this day the most important, was the 1969 study of Long An province by Jeffrey Race, a US Army adviser in South Vietnam who compiled one of the most important documentary records. The most recent to appear is a 1991 study of Hau Nghia province by Eric Bergerud. These studies focus on two critically important provinces in the Delta near Saigon, which were typical of much of the areas of insurgency; both studies review the larger context as well, and reach conclusions not seriously questioned elsewhere, apart from tactical judgments.[29]

Both analysts recognize that the US-imposed regime had no legitimacy in the countryside, where 80 percent of the population lived (and little enough in the urban areas); and that only force could compensate for this lack. Both report that by 1965, when the US war against South Vietnam moved to sheer devastation, the VC had won the war in the provinces they studied, with little external support. Race observes that "the government terrorized far more than did the revolutionary movement—for example, by liquidations of former Vietminh, by artillery and ground attacks on 'communist villages,' and by roundups of 'communist sympathizers.' Yet it was just these tactics that led to the constantly increasing strength of the revolutionary movement in Long An from 1960 to 1965." Prior to 1960, the Diem regime enjoyed a near monopoly of violence and pursued the conflict "through its relentless reprisal against any opposition, its use of torture," and other severe repression, while the Communist Party, "at great cost," kept to "an almost entirely defensive role." When violence was authorized in self-defense, the VC qickly took over the province, parts of which were declared a free strike zone in 1964. US troops took over and vastly increased the violence in 1965. The first North Vietnamese units appeared in 1968.

GVN officials were aware that "communist cadres are close to the people, while ours are not," but never understood why.

They failed entirely to address the needs of the rural masses, in contrast with the revolutionary forces, who "offered concrete and practical solutions to the daily problems of substantial segments of the rural population..." The only recourse was terror, then the incomparable greater violence of the invaders.

Bergerud's conclusions are similar. The Government "lacked legitimacy with the rural peasantry," while "the great strength of the Communist-led National Liberation Front...which enjoyed widespread support among the peasantry,...frustrated allied efforts," as did the unwillingness of the GVN or the US to propose any "fundamental change in the social or economic makeup of South Vietnam." The basic problem was the "extremely formidable political apparatus" of the NLF, their "extremely popular" programs that "earned for the Viet Minh the loyalty and gratitude of hundreds of thousands of poor peasants," many of whom had supported the Viet Minh for generations and had "learned from early childhood to view reality through the prism of Viet Cong ideas, beliefs and prejudices," anthropologist-adviser Gerald Hickey observed in1962. US-GVN terror and violence only increased the "peasantry's deep hatred" for the client regime.

"In harsh reality, activists in rural Vietnam willing 'to help build an effective local government system and support and defend that system' [as advocated by US advisers] were almost exclusively on the side of the Front," which had constructive programs that the US and its clients could not emulate without eroding their own power. "There can be no doubt that...the Front had a virtual lock on the 'best and brightest' of the rural youth," "the support of the most politically aware and most determined segment of the peasantry," and that only "the Front and not the GVN possessed legitimacy in much of rural Vietnam." By the end of 1965, "the NLF had won the war in Hau Nghia province." The CIA representative there concluded that "98 percent of the insurgents in the province were local and that they neither got nor needed substantial aid from Hanoi," even producing their own weapons locally. When the US 25th Infantry Division took over in January 1966, "Hau Nghia was controlled almost entirely by the NLF and had been for some time."

With the US takeover of the war, the legitimacy of the Front if anything increased. By 1966, its followers "could claim very plausibly that they were defending national sovereignty"—against US aggressors, though the inference cannot be drawn. "Manpower and food for the Front came from the hamlets themselves," while the US 25th Division, then rampaging through the province, of course "had to import everything." ARVN was hardly more than a mercenary force. "Given the local sentiment," US-run "programs leading toward economic betterment had to come from the outside," and were "an abject failure"; not surprising, given estimates in some of the targeted areas that about 70 percent of the population were pro-NLF, and only 1 percent openly supported the government, the rest being neutral.

The situation in Laos was similar. The problem there, Hilsman writes, was that "the Communist Pathet Lao were busy drumming up popular support in the two northern provinces, and there were some fears that they would launch a military offensive—although in retrospect the threat seems more likely to have been an expansion of political control based on winning peasant support in the villages." The "threat" was revealed in the 1958 elections. Despite extensive US efforts to subvert them, 9 Pathet Lao (NLHS) candidates and 4 "left-leaning neutralists" were elected (along with 5 right-wingers and 3 non-party delegates), and the leading NLHS figure, Prince Souphanouvong, received more votes than any other candidate. The US was therefore compelled to overthrow the government, placing the ultra-right in power and running elections rigged so crudely that even the most pro-US observers were appalled, while the State Department conceded that the NLHS was "in a position to take over the entire country" by 1961 because of their effective organizing. Hilsman held that "pro-Western, anti-Communist neutrality"—a revealing concept, standard in the literature—"might be the most that could be expected from a country like Laos."[30]

In the face of these bitter realities in South Vietnam, Bergerud continues, the US had only one option: violence. For Kennedy and his circle, violence raised at most tactical problems; the client regime understood that there was no other choice, despite the negative impact on villagers when Diem's agents "beheaded suspects in neighboring hamlets" and otherwise murdered, tortured, and destroyed. "Pacification activities in Hau Nghia were basically coercive in nature from the very beginning, despite 'revolutionary' programs or rhetoric coming from CORDS [the "hearts and minds" contingent] or the GVN. Force, much of it coming from the U.S. Army, was always the key component." "Almost all 'progress' was coercive," and "essentially negative," aimed merely at "military attrition" of the indigenous resistance. In February 1965, the US began regular bombing of Front zones in Hau Nghia, which "were early and frequent targets of the B-52s," with their massive and indiscriminate destruction. By the time the 25th Division arrived, "most free fire zones had become largely depopulated." Crop destruction and other defoliation operations were undertaken from 1962 in the hope they "would force villagers to leave Front areas and move to regions that had a GVN presence and were thus safe from spraying." From the outset, "anything of importance that was accomplished…was due to coercion and violence, most of it supplied by U.S. forces."

The coercion and violence had their successes. Crop destruction and other atrocities caused peasants to flee to "safety." "The huge number of Front followers killed, wounded, captured, or driven to surrender shook the Front very badly." And the US military campaign did cause "great destruction and much loss of innocent life," removing much of the population to "safety" as "Slowly the hamlets were eaten away by small VC initiated incidents and massive U.S. retaliation" (civilian adviser Ollie Davidson). The post-Tet pacification campaign, with its virtually unrestrained terror, finally produced "favorable trends." ("High Tide for the Allies: 1970" is the chapter heading.)

But it came too late. "Unfortunately for the United States, the long war of attrition required to weaken the NLF was simultaneously a crushing burden on the U.S. Army and led inevitably to a steady decline in public support for the war effort" in the US, while dissolving the remnants of the client regime.

As the rhetoric indicates, these are not the reflections of a dove. Bergerud begins by informing the reader that he accepts "the moral validity...of the Vietnam war." His commitment is so firm that no other position is even thinkable. Thus in his review of the "large number of interesting books and articles...concerning the American conduct of the Vietnam War," all, without exception, share his unwavering faith in the "moral validity" of the US effort, differing only on how the noble cause should have been implemented.

It may be true that the Front had "gained moral ascendancy" in Vietnam, could fairly claim to be defending "national sovereignty" against the US aggressors, could easily have won the political victory it sought, and was even able to win military victory before the total takeover by the invading superpower, which could respond to its political strength and popular support only by extraordinary terror and violence. But there can be no question of the "moral validity" of the US cause. "Only American military intervention offered hope for the future" after the Front had won control of the province, Bergerud concludes, "hope" being identified with victory by the aggressors and the local thugs they imposed. Furthermore, "the Front was ruthless in its tactics, unquestionably more so than the GVN," a conclusion that follows at once from the fact that the vastly greater terror and violence of the US clients was in a righteous cause; the US, by definition, cannot be "ruthless," however murderous and destructive, just as it cannot lack "moral validity," whatever it does.

Despite such axioms—which are familiar through the 500-year conquest, and can readily be duplicated in Stalinist and Nazi archives—Bergerud remains an honest historian, whose contributions are of value not only in thoroughly refuting his judgments, but also in baring the reality with telling clarity.

It would be unfair to leave the impression that Bergerud is extreme in these attitudes. He does not approach Guenter Lewy, who he much admires; or Sidney Hook, or Leo Cherne, or other really extreme advocates of state terror and atrocities. And as already noted, and shown in far greater detail elsewhere, the most liberal and humane sectors of intellectual opinion do not depart from these assumptions in any fundamental way. It is "clear," the *New York Times* proclaims, that "the lesson of Vietnam was a sense of the limits of United States power." "Clear," and subject to no discussion. In contrast, the lesson of Afghanistan was not "a sense of the limits of Soviet power," except, perhaps, to some utterly unreconstructed Stalinists. Discussing with much approval the "heroic tale" of a Vietnamese collaborator with the French imperialists and their American successors, the *Times* reviewer describes the methods he devised in 1962 to destroy the "political organization" of the South Vietnamese revolutionaries. The most successful device was to send "counter-terror teams to track down and capture or kill recalcitrant Vietcong officials"—*counter-terror* teams, because it was the US and its clients who were assassinating civilians to undermine an indigenous political organization that they could not confront in the political arena, as fully conceded.[31] The lessons taught by the *Wehrmacht* advisers have been absorbed well beyond Army counterinsurgency manuals, not surprisingly, given their deep roots in the tradition and culture.

Children must be rigorously indoctrinated in these conventions to ensure that Political Correctness will reign unchallenged. The most extensive study of high school history texts found that the word *terror* "does not appear *once* in reference to U.S. or client practices in any of the 48 texts examined in 1979 and 1990. The Viet Cong, it is duly noted, murdered and terrorized; one can only wonder how they could possibly out-terrorize Diem's U.S.-backed forces. "The answer to that question is quite simple: it is true *by definition*, the same device that expunges the vastly greater US terror, and its aggression itself, from the annals of history.[32]

The task of restoring doctrinal conformity among the general population in the post-Vietnam War era has not been an easy one. Considerable effort has been required to entrench a proper understanding of what had happened, and to eradicate the deviant view that the American war was "fundamentally wrong and immoral," not merely a "mistake." This element of the dread "Vietnam syndrome" still infected 71 percent of the population in 1990 (72 percent in 1982, 66 percent in 1986), despite the massive efforts undertaken to overcome the malady, to which educated elites were far less vulnerable. State policies that lose their lustre are reflexively portrayed by respectable intellectuals as a "failed crusade," undertaken for aims that are "noble" but "illusory" and "motivated by the loftiest intentions" (Stanley Karnow's judgment in his best-selling companion volume to a PBS TV series on the war). It is the responsibility of the assassins of history to portray crime as "failure," a mere "aberration," only an apparent departure from our nobility and the perfection of our institutions. Unfortunate consequences are the result of misunderstanding and naiveté, or perhaps the fault of evil men who unaccountably gained inordinate power, soon to be expelled from the body politic.[33]

This much is close to a cultural universal, and the source of much derision when found in enemy states. For the more ex-

treme and humorless Stalinist party hacks, inability to comprehend such Higher Truths demonstrated the "anti-Sovietism" of
the miscreants, a charge that is the very hallmark of a totalitarian
culture and is unknown apart from Stalinist Russia, Brazil under
the Generals, Nazi Germany, and a few other cases, among them
the intellectual mainstream in the United States and its British
counterpart, where books on "Anti-Americanism" are highly
praised and solemnly reviewed by fellow commissars.[34] Outside
of such circles, comparable notions would appear merely comical; consider, for example, the likely reaction in Rome or Milan
to the notion "anti-Italianism"—post-Mussolini, that is.

So effectively has history been rewritten that an informed
journalist at the left-liberal extreme can report that "the US military's distrust of cease-fires [in Iraq] seems to stem from the
Vietnam War," when the Communist enemy—but not, apparently, the US invaders—"used the opportunity [of a bombing
pause] to recover and fight on" (Fred Kaplan). Near the dissident extreme of scholarship, the chairman of the Center for European Studies at Harvard can inform us that Nixon's Christmas
bombing of Hanoi in 1972 "brought the North Vietnamese back
to the conference table" (Stanley Hoffmann). Such fables, long
ago demolished, are alive and well, as the propaganda system has
elegantly recovered; no real problem among the educated classes,
who had rarely strayed from the Party Line. The achievements
of propaganda are well-illustrated by the fact that Americans
generally estimate Vietnamese deaths at about 100,000, a recent
academic study reveals, about 5 percent of the official figure. It
is as if the German public estimated Holocaust deaths at
300,000, the authors note.[35]

What conclusion we would draw about the political culture
of Germany if the public were to believe such an estimate, while
its moral and intellectual leaders declare their righteousness? A
question we might ponder, as Year 501 dawns.

4. Kennedy's Plans and their Import

JFK's aggression was later escalated to a full-scale attack against all of Indochina, becoming one of the most destructive wars of the 500-year conquest. The war also had a long-term impact on the US and global economies, and on political and cultural life. Public indignation over US crimes, though long delayed and never remotely commensurate with their scale, spread to substantial parts of the population. The war stimulated the popular movements of the 1960s, which proliferated and expanded through the Reagan years. The ferment brought previously marginalized sectors into the political arena to pursue their concerns, causing the "crisis of democracy" that liberal elites found so ominous. The ideological institutions of the West have devoted substantial energies to reimposing discipline on a public that was falling out of control, with mixed success. These have been highly significant features of the post-Vietnam years.

The Kennedy-Johnson transition of 1963-1964 assumes a special interest in this connection. It is particularly enlightening to see how Vietnam policies were portrayed by the Kennedy intellectuals at the time, then reinterpreted after the enterprise turned sour and the disaster had to be dated to November 23, 1963 so as to preserve the image of Camelot and the reputations of the courtiers. This is an intriguing chapter of cultural history, still unfolding.

The significance of the issue is enhanced by its alleged relation to the Kennedy assassination, a topic that has aroused much attention and indeed passion, peaking in 1991-1992. In this case, as noted earlier, it is largely grassroots elements (often called "the left"[36]) that have taken up the cudgels in the defense of President Kennedy, on the theory that he was assassinated by powerful groups that perceived him to be a dangerous "radical reformer." These dark forces are variously identified as the CIA, the far right, militarists, etc. Many on the left accept this perception as accurate, holding that JFK was about to withdraw from Vietnam, end the Cold War and the arms race, smash the CIA to a thousand pieces, dismantle the military-industrial complex, and set the country on a course towards peace and justice. Others hold only that the assassins exaggerated his reformist zeal. Some popular variants bring in other assassinations, real and alleged. The plot also becomes intertwined with theories of a "secret team" that has "hijacked the state," bringing us to our current sorry pass.

Quite broadly, the assassination is depicted either as bringing to a close an earlier age of innocence (at least, political legitimacy), or as aborting JFK's plans to lead us toward that condition, in a radical departure from the historical norm. Under either interpretation, the legitimacy of authority was lost in fundamental ways with the assassination, never to be regained, a matter of great importance. These tendencies, which have received strong support from leading Kennedy intellectuals, have come to consume a large part of the limited energies and resources of the left.

Vietnam policies of 1963-1964 play a central role in these conceptions. That is not implausible, given the timing of the assassination and the subsequent escalation. The sense that this was a historical turning point is fortified by other factors: the appeal of Kennedy imagery, the deterioration of the conditions of life for a large part of the population since the early 1970s, the failure of the civil rights movement to realize its early promise, and the growing recognition that the political and economic systems are not responsive to the needs and concerns of the general public.

When Kennedy was assassinated, the war was still at the level of extreme state terror but limited aggression. We then face the central question: Did JFK plan to withdraw without victory? The thesis currently prevalent among Kennedy intellectuals and large segments of the left is that Kennedy was indeed carrying out such a plan, aborted by the assassination, and that Johnson at once reversed this policy and escalated the war; the two groups then part company on what this indicates about the assassination.[37] The thesis is understood to imply that JFK would not have responded to changing conditions in the manner of his closest advisers and war managers.

If true, the thesis is important, lending weight to the belief that Kennedy was indeed a remarkable if not unique figure. If it is groundless, then it becomes reasonable to inquire into the roots of the picture of innocence lost, or prospects destroyed.

Versions of the thesis have reached a wide audience from the late 1960s in books by Kennedy associates and assassination theorists. It became a major national issue with the 1991 release of Oliver Stone's film *JFK*. According to Stone and his colleagues, their primary historical source on Vietnam is a "ten year study" by John Newman, published in 1992 by the conglomerate that produced the film. Presented as a major historical work, Newman's study is the most ambitious effort to defend the withdrawal-without-victory thesis, which he and others take to be established by his research. The film was released with a major publicity campaign, with PR specialist Frank Mankiewicz, Robert Kennedy's former campaign manager, in charge of Washington press relations, and reached a huge audience.

Stone's film elicited a vigorous response, including harsh attacks and favorable reviews, and opinion pieces and letter exchanges across the spectrum, sometimes with considerable passion. Liberal critics tended to support Stone's thesis about JFK, while denouncing him for concocting assassination conspiracies and "[running] away from the serious question, which is why the American policy elite, and the American political class and press, all of them acting with good intentions, should have gone so wrong, and done so much evil" (William Pfaff). The film was granted a rare front-page story in the *New York Times*, reporting the awed response of viewers to "the only shining star that ever crossed the American political sky," and their amazement to learn "what [JFK] might have done, what they stopped"— "they" having the intended ominous ring. Other viewers asked "Why has this been ignored?," suggesting a link to establishment efforts to disguise the truth about the assassination. That the Warren Commission Report is a fraud is assumed by a majority of the population, hardly a surprise, given the enormous publicity the charge has been accorded in the mass media. It is not even surprising to learn that when a faulty transmitter disrupted cable TV service in San Diego, delaying transmission of a film on "the JFK conspiracy," dozens of viewers called the station denouncing this CIA plot. Books condemning the Warren Commission Report dominated the bestseller lists in early 1992, while its critics protested establishment suppression of their skepticism.

Stone's film traced the Kennedy assassination to a high-level conspiracy: CIA, military-industrial complex, and others, perhaps even LBJ. The film, Stone informed the National Press Club, suggests that Kennedy was assassinated "because he was determined to withdraw from and never send combat troops to Vietnam" (that he was "withdrawing from Vietnam" and "had committed himself firmly...to oppose the entry of U.S. combat troops" has been "unequivocally" demonstrated, Stone added, citing Arthur Schlesinger and John Newman). At a Town Hall (New York) forum sponsored by the *Nation*, Norman Mailer told an enthusiastic audience that "If Kennedy was going to end the war in Vietnam, he had to be replaced. Lyndon Johnson was the man to do it." Stone's film presents the "overarching paradigm" for all further inquiry into the assassination, Mailer went on, though not the complete solution to the mysteries surrounding this "huge and hideous event, in which the gods warred and a god fell," a cosmic tragedy that casts its pall over all subsequent history. The judgment, shared by many others, was articulated by the lead actor, Kevin Costner, in his role as the film's hero, New Orleans District Attorney Jim Garrison: "We have all become Hamlets in our country, children of a slain father-leader whose killers still possess the throne."[38]

Newman's book was favorably received, notably, in a prominent review in the *New York Times* by JFK's close associate and chronicler, Arthur Schlesinger, who lauded Newman's scholarship and endorsed his main conclusions, as he did elsewhere as well. Other reviewers also found Newman's argument convincing.[39] These enthusiastic reactions, and Newman's own media interventions, contributed to the 1991-1992 fervor. In a spectrum ranging from the left to leading Kennedy liberals, Newman's book is taken as the basic source establishing the withdrawal-without-victory thesis, with all of its broad implications.

For many reasons, then, it is worthwhile to have a close look at the presidential transition and the issue of withdrawal-escalation. The question of what Kennedy might have done, or what was hidden in the secret recesses of his heart, we may leave to seers and mystics. We can, however, inspect what he did do and say, an inquiry facilitated by a rich documentary record.[40]

5. The Prospects Look Bright

At first, JFK's 1961-1962 aggression appeared to be a grand success. Hilsman's enthusiasm, cited earlier, was widely shared. By late spring of 1962, the *Pentagon Papers* analyst observes, "the prospects looked bright" and "to many the end of the insurgency seemed in sight." The US leadership in Vietnam and Washington "was confident and cautiously optimistic," and "In some quarters, even a measure of euphoria obtained."

In his semi-official history of the Kennedy presidency, Arthur Schlesinger observes that by the end of 1961, "The President unquestionably felt that an American retreat in Asia might upset the whole world balance." The stakes being so enormous, he escalated the conflict in the manner already described. "The result in 1962 was to place the main emphasis on the military effort" in South Vietnam, Schlesinger writes, with "encouraging effects" as "The advisers flocked in with the weapons of modern war, from typewriters to helicopters," helping to plan military actions in which they "sometimes participated themselves." These achievements enabled Kennedy to report in his January 1963 State of the Union message that "The spear point of aggression has been blunted in South Vietnam." In Schlesinger's own words: "1962 had not been a bad year:...aggression checked in Vietnam."[41]

Recall that Kennedy and his historian-associate are describing the year 1962, when Kennedy escalated from extreme terrorism to outright aggression.

This optimistic assessment of the prospects for successful aggression led Robert McNamara to initiate planning for the withdrawal of US forces from Vietnam, leaving to the client regime the dirty work of cleaning up the remnants. Kennedy and McNamara recognized that domestic support for JFK's war was thin, and that problems might arise if it were to persist too long. The military was divided, but with no interest in staying on after victory. Similarly, in November 1967, General Westmoreland announced that with victory imminent, US troops could begin to withdraw in 1969 (as happened, though under circumstances that he did not anticipate); that recommendation does not show that he was a secret dove.[42] Advocacy of withdrawal after assurance of victory was not a controversial stand.

In contrast, withdrawal *without victory* would have been highly controversial. Within the domestic mainstream, that position received scant support: the first timid editorial advocacy of it, to my knowledge, was in late 1969, well after corporate and political elites had determined that the operation should be liquidated as too costly. When Howard Zinn published a book in

1967 calling for US withdrawal, the idea was considered too out-landish even to discuss.[43]

The question to be considered, then, is whether JFK, despite his 1961-1962 escalation and his militant public stand, planned to withdraw *without* victory, a plan aborted by the assassination, which cleared the way for Lyndon Johnson and his fellow-warmongers to bring on a major war.

6. JFK and Withdrawal: the Early Plans

The major withdrawal decisions were reported at once in the press, and the basic facts about the internal deliberations lying behind them became known 20 years ago, when the *Pentagon Papers* appeared. Discussing the "Vietnam problem" as perceived in July 1962, the analyst writes that "At the behest of the President, the Secretary of Defense undertook to reexamine the situation there and address himself to its future—with a view to assuring that it be brought to a successful conclusion within a reasonable time." At a July 23 "full-dress conference" in Honolulu, McNamara was impressed with the "tremendous progress" that had been made (his words). He called for "phasing out major U.S. advisory and logistic support activities." MACV Commander General Paul Harkins estimated that the VC should be "eliminated as a significant force" about a year after the Vietnamese forces then being trained and equipped "became fully operational." McNamara, however, insisted upon "a conservative view": planning should be based on the assumption that "it would take three years instead of one, that is, by the latter part of 1965." He also "observed that it might be difficult to retain public support for U.S. operations in Vietnam indefinitely," a constant concern. Therefore, it was necessary "to phase out U.S. military involvement." On July 26, the Joint Chiefs ordered preparation of a Comprehensive Plan for South Vietnam to implement McNamara's decisions. The stated objective was to ensure that by the end of 1965, the Saigon government would take over "without the need for continued U.S. special military assistance." The crucial operating assumption was that "The insurgency will be under control" by the end of 1965.

On January 25, 1963, the Comprehensive Plan was presented to the Joint Chiefs. General Harkins's plan stated that "the phase-out of the US special military assistance is envisioned as generally occurring during the period July 1965-June 1966," earlier where feasible.[44]

A few days later, the Chiefs were reassured that this was the right course by a report by a JCS investigative team headed by Army Chief of Staff Earle Wheeler that included leading military hawks. The team had been "asked to form a military judgment as to the prospects for a successful conclusion of the conflict in a reasonable period of time." Its report was generally upbeat and optimistic: "the Government of Vietnam is making steady and favorable progress" in the US-guided military offensive, and the "common people" show increased confidence that "the government is going to triumph." A new "National Campaign Plan" ("Operation Explosion") is in place, assigning "greater initiative" to the Saigon army than in the past, a counterpart to the MACV Comprehensive Plan "designed to prepare the armed forces of South Vietnam to exercise control of their territory, without our help, by the end of calendar year 1965." Prospects for both were hopeful. Their anticipated success would allow a "concurrent phase-out of United States support personnel, leaving a Military Assistance Advisory Group [MAAG] of a strength of about 1,600 personnel." All of this was considered feasible and appropriate by the top military command.

Technical suggestions were presented to implement these plans, including a recommendation to relax the rules of engagement for US armed helicopters, already deployed "in an escort role, under combat conditions"; they should be allowed to attack

"Viet Cong targets of opportunity, in a combat situation," even
if not fired upon. US Farmgate operations, disguised with Vietnam Air Force markings, already had such authority under
Kennedy's war. Another recommendation was to go beyond "the
minor intelligence and sabotage forays [1 line not declassified]"
to "a coordinated program of sabotage, destruction, propaganda,
and subversive missions against North Vietnam," keeping the US
"wholly in the background while at the same time conducting the
anti-North Vietnam campaign as a powerful military endeavor
rather than as an ancillary [1 line not declassified]." Wheeler's
team recommended that the US should "intensify" the training
of Vietnamese military forces for these missions "and encourage
their execution of raids and sabotage missions in North Vietnam,
coordinated with other military operations" [another two and a
half lines not declassified].

Wheeler then reported directly to the President on February 1, informing him "that things were going well in Vietnam militarily, but that 'Ho Chi Minh was fighting the war for peanuts
and if we ever expected to win that affair out there, we had to
make him bleed a little bit'." The President "was quite interested
in this," General Wheeler recalled in oral history (July 1964). His
dovish advisers were also impressed. In April 1963, on assuming
the position of Assistant Secretary of State for Far Eastern Affairs, Roger Hilsman proposed to "continue the covert, or at least
deniable, operations along the general lines we have been following for some months" against North Vietnam with the objective
of "keeping the threat of eventual destruction alive in Hanoi's
mind." But "significant action against North Vietnam" is unwise
on tactical grounds: it should be delayed until "we have demonstrated success in our counter-insurgency program." "Premature
action" against the North might also "so alarm our friends and
allies and a significant segment of domestic opinion that the
pressures for neutralization will become formidable"; as always,

the dread threat of diplomacy must be deflected. With judicious planning, Hilsman said, "I believe we can win in Viet-Nam."[45]

We thus learn that in January 1963, in an atmosphere of great optimism, the military initiatives for withdrawal went hand-in-hand with plans for escalation of the war within South Vietnam and possibly intensified operations against North Vietnam. We learn further that "intelligence and sabotage forays" into North Vietnam were already underway—since mid-1962, according to JFK's National Security adviser McGeorge Bundy. On December 11, 1963, as the new Administration took over, Forrestal confirmed that "For some time the Central Intelligence Agency has been engaged in joint clandestine operations with ARVN against North Vietnam." Journalist William Pfaff reports that in the summer of 1962, at a Special Forces encampment north of Saigon he observed a CIA "patrol loading up in an unmarked C-46 with a Chinese pilot in civilian clothes," taking off for a mission in North Vietnam ("possibly into China itself"); "Some were Asians, some Americans or Europeans," who "certainly were not going north to give advice."[46]

The connection between withdrawal and escalation is readily understandable: successful military actions would make it possible for the GVN to take over the task from the Americans, who could then withdraw with victory secured, satisfying the common intent of the extreme hawks, war manager McNamara, and JFK.

The same natural connection was established in 1968-1969, when an authentic withdrawal was initiated. It was combined with the most devastating and ferocious campaign of mass murder yet undertaken by the US expeditionary force, though downplayed by the cultural managers in favor of incidents that could be treated as "aberrations" by GIs in the field. The withdrawal was also accompanied by a huge expansion of the assault against the civilian societies of Laos and Cambodia, also suppressed by the loyal media, who falsely accused Richard Nixon of deceiving them about the slaughter and the decisive US role in it, when he fell out of favor. Again, the association is a natural one: withdrawal is conditioned on victory.[47]

Not everyone was as optimistic as the military command. A few days before the President heard Wheeler's upbeat report, he received a memorandum from Hilsman and Forrestal (January 25) that was more qualified. They condemned the press for undue pessimism and underplaying US success, and agreed that "The war in South Vietnam is clearly going better than it was a year ago." They praised ARVN's "increased aggressiveness" resulting from the US military escalation, reporting that GVN control now extended to over half the rural population (compared with 8 percent under VC control), a considerable gain through late 1962. But "the negative side of the ledger is still awesome." The VC have increased their regular forces, recruiting locally and supplied locally, and are "extremely effective." "Thus the conclusion seems inescapable that the Viet Cong could continue the war effort at the present level, or perhaps increase it, even if the infiltration routes were completely closed." "Our overall judgment, in sum, is that we are probably winning, but certainly more slowly than we had hoped." They made a variety of technical recommendations to implement the counterinsurgency program more efficiently, with more direct US involvement; and to improve the efficiency of the US mission to accelerate the "Progress toward winning the war."[48]

The 1963 assumptions were to come into far more serious question after the US-backed coup that replaced the Diem-Nhu regime on November 1. High-level civilian and military officials finally came to recognize that their optimism was based on fraudulent reports. It became increasingly clear that the crucial condition for the withdrawal plans—that victory be assured—no longer obtained. Through 1964, the situation continued to deteriorate. Calls for actions against the North then increased, but on different grounds than in early 1963: with the US position collapsing in the South, the last hope was to coerce the DRV to order the southern insurgents to desist. From 1965, the US took the war over directly in the South and expanded it to a full-scale attack on the rest of Indochina as well. The dovish alternative was an "enclave strategy" with the US troop level frozen at under 100,000 men.

Returning to the period of optimism, on April 18, 1963, the Director of the State Department's Vietnam Working Group, Chalmers Wood, recommended that "We should veto any further requests for increases [in troop level]...and quietly support McNamara's intention to achieve a significant reduction by the end of the year, provided things go well." He felt that "1,000 military could be pulled out of Saigon tomorrow and things would go better." He recommended "that a substantial number of American military should be pulled out of Viet-Nam by the end of this year, provided we make the progress suggested by [Brigadier Robert] Thompson," the respected head of the British Advisory Mission. Thompson had recommended to McNamara that "if progress during 1963 continued good," it might be wise to withdraw about 1,000 men.

On May 6, McNamara stated that military advisers should be the last category removed, and requested a plan for withdrawal of "1,000 or so personnel late this year [1963] if the situation allows." Secretary of State Dean Rusk approved (May 13), as did Chairman of the Joint Chiefs Maxwell Taylor (August 20), Kennedy's most trusted military adviser. The "fundamental objective" remains unchanged, Michael Forrestal advised the President on August 27: the US must "give wholehearted support to the prosecution of the war against the Viet Cong terrorists," and "continue assistance to any government in South Vietnam which shows itself capable of sustaining this effort."[49]

The reference to "any government" relates to the increasing concerns of the Kennedy Administration over the Diem regime.

One problem was that its repression was evoking internal resistance, which was interfering with the war effort. Another was that
Diem and his brother Nhu, considered "the power behind the
throne," were pressing their demands for US withdrawal with increasing urgency. On April 22, the CIA had reported that Diem
and Nhu "were concerned over recent 'infringements' of Vietnamese sovereignty," and "after building up a strong case,
[Diem] plans to confront Ambassador Nolting and USMACV
Chief General Harkins with irrefutable evidence of U.S. responsibility, demanding a reduction in the number of U.S. personnel
in South Vietnam on the basis that the force is too large and un-
manageable." A week earlier, a source (not declassified) had reported that in an April 12 conversation, Nhu "repeated his view
that it would be useful to reduce the numbers of Americans by
anywhere from 500 to 3,000 or 4,000." In a front-page interview
in the *Washington Post*, May 12, Nhu stated that "South Viet
Nam would like to see half of the 12,000 to 13,000 American
military stationed here leave the country."[50]

Administration planners feared that the GVN pressures for
withdrawal of US forces would become difficult to resist, a danger enhanced by exploratory GVN efforts to reach a diplomatic
settlement with the North. The skimpy political base for
Kennedy's war would then erode, and the US would be compelled to withdraw without victory. That option being unacceptable to JFK and his advisers, the Saigon regime had to get on
board, or be dismissed.

7. JFK and Withdrawal: the Dénouement

By the end of August, JFK and his most dovish advisers (Averell
Harriman, Roger Hilsman, George Ball) agreed that the client
government should be overthrown. On August 28, the President
"asked the Defense Department to come up with ways of building
up the anti-Diem forces in Saigon." He called for actions "which

would maximize the chances of the rebel generals" and said, "We should ask Ambassador Lodge and General Harkins how we can build up military forces which would carry out a coup." Harriman said that without a coup, "we cannot win the war" and "must withdraw." Hilsman "agreed that we cannot win the war unless Diem is removed," as did Ball, while Robert Kennedy also called for efforts to strengthen the rebel generals. Secretary Rusk warned JFK that "Nhu might call on the North Vietnamese to help him throw out the Americans." Hilsman urged (August 30) that if Diem and Nhu make any "Political move toward the DRV (such as opening of neutralization negotiations)," or even hint at such moves, we should "Encourage the generals to move promptly with a coup," and undertake "military action" if the DRV tries to counter our actions, letting them "know unequivocally that we shall hit the DRV with all that is necessary to force it to desist," bringing in "U.S. combat forces to assist the coup group to achieve victory," if necessary. "The important thing is to win the war," Hilsman advised McGeorge Bundy; and that meant getting rid of the Saigon regime, which was dragging its feet and looking for ways out. The President concurred that "our primary objective remains winning war," Rusk cabled to the Saigon Embassy.

The CIA had been reporting for months "that Nhu policy was one of ultimate neutralization and unification of Vietnam," in accord with the 1954 Geneva agreements, and continued to warn that "the GVN, the DRV, and the French may have been engaged of late in exploring the possibilities of some kind of North-South rapprochement," which might lead to a GVN demand for US withdrawal (September 26). In a September 30 memorandum, William Sullivan reviewed a long discussion with the French Chargé in Saigon and the Canadian and Indian International Control Commission (ICC) officials. They discounted current rumors about North-South dealings, but "all of them insisted that we should not discount the possibility of such a deal in the future," perhaps "three or four months," the well-informed French Chargé felt. Such reports could only increase the alarm in Washington, intensifying the fear of a peaceful settlement.[51]

Particularly disquieting was a public statement of August 29 by French President Charles de Gaulle, expressing the hope that the Vietnamese "could go ahead with their activities independently of the outside, in internal peace and unity and in harmony with their neighbors." In a memorandum preparing the President for a September 2 TV interview with Walter Cronkite, McGeorge Bundy focused JFK's attention on de Gaulle's statement, while advising that he continue to "ignore Nosey Charlie." He warned against the "specter of neutralist solution," reviewing de Gaulle's apparent belief "in neutralizing Vietnam" and advising JFK to express incomprehension, calling instead for France "to share in the work of resisting Communist aggression in Vietnam." Kennedy followed Bundy's advice. When Cronkite asked about the de Gaulle statement, he responded that the US had "listened" but without interest, indeed, with irritation:

> What, of course, makes Americans somewhat impatient is that after carrying this load for 18 years, we are glad to get counsel, but we would like a little more assistance, real assistance. But we are going to meet our responsibility anyway. It doesn't do us any good to say, "Well, why don't we all just go home and leave the world to those who are our enemies."

Kennedy reiterated his resentment in private. In a White House conference the next day (September 3), he asked "what the French are doing toward assisting the Vietnamese." After being shown a paper on the subject, "The President commented that the French were trying to get for Vietnam what had been done in Laos, i.e., neutralization," which "was not working in Laos" and was no model for Vietnam. He also wondered why Walter Lippmann proposed the Laotian model. Asked whether France would protest his comments about de Gaulle in the Cronkite interview, "the President said he doubted [French]

Ambassador Alphand had the guts to protest." JFK remained adamant in his opposition to a diplomatic settlement that would entail withdrawal without victory.[52]

The consensus remained that "the war in the countryside is going well now" (Ambassador Lodge, September 11), though discordant notes were being sounded. There was substantial urban unrest, and the Diem government was not considered trustworthy. In a September 11 paper, Hilsman wrote that "The U.S. policy objective should continue to be the maintenance of a viable, strong and free area in South Viet-Nam capable of maintaining its independence, successfully resisting Communist aggression, and susceptible to U.S. influence." Accordingly, "we should tell Diem that we are ready to prosecute our program to annihilate the Viet Cong menace with renewed vigor and that we expect full cooperation from him in this endeavor"—or else. Diem must "focus on winning the war," Hilsman added in a September 16 memorandum.

This memorandum outlined a plan that the President had requested in the light of Diem's recalcitrance. Delivered to the President on that day, Hilsman's plan stated that "Withdrawal by the U.S. would be immediately disastrous to the war effort." To attain our "overall objective," which is "to win the war against the Viet Cong," we must support "what helps win the war" and "oppose" what "interferes with the war effort," in accord with the "policy guideline" that the President had stated on September 12 (see page 58).[53]

The general assessment was that the war could not be won "if Nhu remains in power" (Joseph Mendenhall, also considered a dove). Worse yet, Nhu "has frequently claimed that the American presence must be reduced," the CIA reported, and was continuing his dealings with the North, which might lead to a peaceful settlement, undermining Kennedy's war policies.

The basic principle, unquestioned, is that we must "focus on winning the war." On September 14, Harriman wrote to Lodge, making the point unmistakeable: "I can assure you that from the President on down everybody is determined to support you and the country team in winning the war against the Viet Cong. There may be some differences in opinion or in emphasis as to how it is to be done, but there are no quitters here."[54]

In particular, JFK is no quitter. There is not a phrase in the internal record to suggest that this judgment by a trusted high-level Kennedy adviser, at the dovish extreme, should be qualified in any way.

We now approach the final weeks of JFK's presidency, the last opportunity to determine his intentions. We therefore pay close attention to his (limited) involvement in discussion and decision-making.

On September 17, after a meeting with his NSC advisers to discuss the plan for military victory that Hilsman had prepared, President Kennedy instructed Ambassador Lodge to pressure Diem to "get everyone back to work and get them to focus on winning the war," repeating his regular emphasis on victory. It was particularly important to show military progress because "of need to make effective case with Congress for continued prosecution of the effort," the President added, expressing his constant concern that congressional support for his commitment to military victory was weak. "To meet these needs," he informed Lodge, he was sending his top aides McNamara and Taylor to Vietnam. Their mission was to appraise "the military and paramilitary effort to defeat the Viet Cong," JFK instructed McNamara, and to ensure "the progress of the contest," a matter of "the first importance." There have been "heartening results" until recently, but "future effectiveness" requires new actions by the GVN and Washington. The goal remains "the winning of the war," the President again emphasized, adding that "The way to confound the press is to win the war." Like Congress, the press was an enemy because of its lack of enthusiasm for a war to victory and its occasional calls for diplomacy.

Taylor proposed that he and McNamara present Diem with a fixed time scale within which "the war must be won." According to McGeorge Bundy's minutes, "The President did not say 'yes' or 'no' to this proposal," apparently unwilling to be bound by any commitment to withdraw.[55]

McNamara and Taylor were encouraged by what they found. Taylor informed Diem that he was "convinced that the Viet Cong insurgency in the north and center can be reduced to little more than sporadic incidents by the end of 1964" and the war effort everywhere should be "completed by the end of 1965." On October 2, Taylor and McNamara presented this analysis to the President, noting that "The military campaign has made great progress and continues to progress." On these assumptions, they presented a series of recommendations, three of which were later authorized (watered down a bit) in NSAM 263:

- "An increase in the military tempo" throughout the country so that the military campaign in the Northern and Central areas will be over by the end of 1964, and in the South (the Delta) by the end of 1965.
- Vietnamese should be trained to take over "essential functions now performed by U.S. military personnel" by the end of 1965, so that "It should be possible to withdraw the bulk of U.S. personnel by that time."
- In accordance with point two, "the Defense Department should announce in the very near future presently prepared plans to withdraw 1000 U.S. military personnel by the end of 1963. This action should be explained in low key as an initial step in a long-term program to replace U.S. personnel with trained Vietnamese without impairment of the war effort."

Their report stressed again that the "overriding objective" is victory, a matter "vital to United States security." They repeated that withdrawal could not be too long delayed: "any significant slowing in the rate of progress would surely have a serious effect on U.S. popular support for the U.S. effort." They expressed their belief "that the U.S. part of the task can be completed by the end of 1965," at which time military victory would have been assured. The withdrawal plans were crucially qualified in the usual way: "No further reductions should be made until the requirements of the 1964 campaign become firm," that is, until battlefield success is assured.[56]

Note that JFK and his advisers consistently regarded lack of popular support for the war and GVN initiatives toward political settlement not as an opportunity for withdrawal, but rather as a threat to victory.

The National Security Council met the same day to consider these proposals. The President's role was, as usual, marginal. He repeated that "the major problem was with U.S. public opinion" and again balked at the time scale. He opposed a commitment to withdraw some forces in 1963 because "if we were not able to take this action by the end of this year, we would be accused of being over optimistic." McNamara, in contrast, "saw great value in this sentence in order to meet the view of Senator Fulbright and others that we are bogged down forever in Vietnam." The phrase was left as "a part of the McNamara-Taylor report rather than as predictions of the President," who thus remained uncommitted to withdrawal, at his insistence.

A public statement was released to the press, presenting the McNamara-Taylor judgment that "the major part of the U.S. military task can be completed by the end of 1965, although there may be a continuing requirement for a limited number of U.S. training personnel," and that the training program "should have progressed to the point" where 1,000 men can be withdrawn by the end of the year. The statement repeated the standard position that the US will work with the GVN "to deny this country to Communism and to suppress the externally stimulated and supported insurgency of the Viet Cong as promptly as possible," continuing with "Major U.S. assistance in support of this military effort," which "is needed only until the insurgency has been suppressed or until the national security forces of the Government of South Viet-Nam are capable of suppressing it."[57]

At a White House conference on October 5, the President directed that the decision to remove 1,000 US advisers "should not be raised formally with Diem. Instead the action should be carried out routinely as part of our general posture of withdrawing people when they are no longer needed."

The results of this meeting were formalized as NSAM 263 (October 11), a brief statement in which "The President approved the three military recommendations cited above...," weakened by one change: that "no formal announcement be made of the implementation of plans to withdraw 1000 U.S. military personnel by the end of 1963." The final provision of NSAM 263 is JFK's personal approval of a telegram instructing Ambassador Lodge to "increase effectiveness of war effort" along with training and arming of new forces, so as to enhance the prospects for victory, on which withdrawal was conditioned. It is necessary, the telegram adds, to overcome the "crisis of confidence among Vietnamese people which is eroding popular support for GVN that is vital for victory," and the "crisis of confidence on the part of the American public and Government," who also do not see how "our actions are related to our fundamental objective of victory."[58]

Note that read literally, NSAM 263 says very little. It approves the McNamara-Taylor recommendations to intensify the war and military training so that "It should be possible to withdraw the bulk of U.S. personnel" by the end of 1965, and includes

JFK's personal instructions to Lodge to intensify military action to achieve "our fundamental objective of victory." It does not call for implementing a 1,000-man withdrawal, but rather endorses the third point of the McNamara-Taylor proposal concerning plans for such withdrawal "as an initial step in a long-term program" to be conducted "without impairment of the war effort," deleting their call for formal announcement of these plans.

Presumably, the intent was to implement the withdrawal plans if military conditions allow, but that intent is unstated. The fact might be borne in mind in light of elaborate later efforts to read great significance into nuances of phrasing so as to demonstrate a dramatic change in policy with the Kennedy-Johnson transition. Adopting these interpretive techniques, we would conclude that NSAM 263 is almost vacuous. I stress that is not my interpretation; I assume the obvious unstated intention, only suggesting that other documents be treated in the same reasonable manner—in which case, widely-held beliefs will quickly evaporate.

As noted, the basic decisions were made public at once. The picture presented then requires no significant modification in light of the huge mass of documents now available, though these make much more clear the President's unwillingness to commit himself to the withdrawal recommended by his war managers, his concern that domestic opinion might not stay the course, his insistence that withdrawal be conditioned on military victory, and his orders to step up the military effort and to "maximize the chances of the rebel generals" to replace the Diem regime by one that will "focus on winning" and not entertain thoughts of US withdrawal and peaceful settlement.

Robert Kennedy also had reservations about making the withdrawal plan public. He felt that we were "so deeply committed to the support of the effort in Vietnam that Diem will not be greatly influenced" by the announced plan (one of its purposes being to press Diem onwards with the war effort). At a White House Staff meeting on October 7, Bundy noted that reservations had been voiced about the withdrawal, expressing his surprise that "some people were taking as 'pollyanna-ish' the 'McNamara-Taylor' statement that we could pull out of Vietnam in two years." He stated that the "general line" for a forthcoming presidential press conference "will be that in two years the Vietnamese will be able to finish the job without US military forces on the scene—a position considered reasonable by everyone around the table" (Bundy, Forrestal, Generals Taylor and Clifton [JFK's military aide] are mentioned).[59]

Through October, problems with the GVN continued to mount. Nhu openly called for the Americans to depart, saying that he and his brother had opposed the American intervention at "the time of greatest danger" in 1961-1962, and now wanted US troops out completely. The US should only provide aid, he demanded. Ambassador Lodge warned that "we should consider a request to withdraw as a growing possibility."

Another problem was the lack of "effectiveness of GVN in its relation to its own people." Asked about this, Lodge responded in an "Eyes only for the President" communication that "Viet-Nam is not a thoroughly strong police state...because, unlike Hitler's Germany, it is not efficient" and is thus unable to suppress the "large and well-organized underground opponent strongly and ever-freshly motivated by vigorous hatred." The Vietnamese "appear to be more than ever anxious to be left alone," and though they "are said to be capable of great violence on occasion," "there is no sight of it at the present time," another impediment to US efforts. The same concerns were expressed about the Indonesian Generals at the same time, though they proved equal to the task, gaining much esteem for their Nazi-style ruthlessness. The Saigon Generals, however, were never able to meet Washington standards.[60]

Small wonder that JFK was unwilling to commit himself to the McNamara-Taylor withdrawal proposal. Note that the same defects of the US clients underlie the critique of the strategic hamlet program by Kennedy doves (see page 68).

Intelligence continued to report that the optimistic projections were dubious while pressures for unification and neutralization remained strong. Paul Kattenburg, at the dovish fringe, reported yet another problem: "Chemical defoliation and crop destruction operations are effective weapons against the VC," but "Present approval procedures are too cumbersome" and "The psychological and civic action aspects of the operation are not particularly good." The need is for more efficiency and better PR.[61]

Washington's coup plans continued, with Ambassador Lodge in operational command. The only hesitation was fear of failure. JFK thought that we "could lose our entire position in Southeast Asia overnight" if the coup plans failed. When the coup finally took place on November 1, replacing Diem and Nhu (who were killed) by a military regime, the President praised Lodge effusively for his "fine job" and "leadership," an "achievement...of the greatest importance" that "is recognized here throughout the Government." With the generals now in power, "our primary emphasis should be on effectiveness rather than upon external appearances," the President added. We must help the coup regime to confront "the real problems of winning the contest against the Communists and holding the confidence of its own people." The "ineffectiveness, loss of popular confidence, and the prospect of defeat that were decisive in shaping our relations to the Diem regime" are now a thing of the past, the President hoped, thanks to Lodge's inspired leadership and coup-management, with its gratifying outcome (November 6).[62]

Two weeks before Kennedy's assassination, there is not a phrase in the voluminous internal record that even hints at withdrawal without victory. JFK urges that everyone "focus on win-

ning the war"; withdrawal is conditioned on victory, and motivated by domestic discontent with Kennedy's war. The stakes are
considered enormous. Nothing substantial changes as the mantle
passes to LBJ.

The post-coup situation had positive and negative aspects
from the point of view of the President and his advisers. On the
positive side, they hoped that the ruling generals would now at
last focus on victory as the President had demanded, gain popular
support, and end the irritating calls for US withdrawal and moves
towards a peaceful settlement. On the other hand, there was dis-
array at all levels, while at home, advocacy of diplomacy was not
stilled. The dovish advisers stressed the need to counter these tendencies. Mendenhall warned Hilsman about the danger posed by
suggestions in the *New York Times* (November 6, 10) "that the
U.S. should undertake international negotiations for settlement
of the Vietnam problem." He proposed a private meeting with
the editors "to try to set them straight on the situation in Vietnam
and on U.S. policy regarding Vietnam." On November 13, Forrestal informed *Times* editor Robert Kleiman that "it would be
folly" to consider a negotiated settlement: "South Vietnam was
still not strong enough to approach the bargaining table with any
hope of coming away whole," and "responsible Vietnamese *in Vietnam*" would probably view such prospects as "a complete sellout
by the U.S." He advised Bundy that we should prepare "to
counter" further efforts "to peddle" this idea in the media.[63]

Meanwhile, evidence that undermined the optimistic assessments was becoming harder to ignore. A week after the coup,
State Department Intelligence, with the concurrence of the CIA,
reported that by late October the military situation had sharply
deteriorated, predicting "unfavorable end-1963 values" for its statistical factors. The new government confirmed that the GVN
"had been losing the war against the VC in the Delta for some
time because it had been losing the population." A top-level meet-

ing was held in Honolulu on November 20 to consider the next steps. The US mission in Vietnam recommended that the withdrawal plans be maintained, the new government being "warmly disposed toward the U.S." and offering "opportunities to exploit that we never had before." Kennedy's plans to escalate the assault against the southern resistance could now be implemented, with a stable regime finally in place. McNamara, ever cautious, stressed that "South Vietnam is under tremendous pressure from the VC," noting a sharp increase in VC incidents after the coup, and urged that "We must be prepared to devote enough resources to this job of winning the war to be certain of accomplishing it..." At an 8 AM White House meeting on November 22, Bundy was informed that "for the first time" military reporting was "realistic about the situation in the Delta."[64]

Before proceeding, let us have a look at what was publicly available in the press at once. The topic merits a brief review, in the light of later allegations about media suppression. That distortion and suppression by the media are common is not in doubt. But not in this case, it turns out. I will keep to the *New York Times*.

The October 2 McNamara-Taylor military recommendations that are (largely) authorized in NSAM 263 were outlined in the lead story in the *New York Times* the next day. The story correctly describes the National Security Council decisions, and is accompanied by the text of the White House statement. In conformity to the internal record, the withdrawal plans are attributed to McNamara and Taylor, not JFK.

In a news conference of October 31, published the next day, JFK maintained the caution he showed in internal discussion, distancing himself from the withdrawal plans:

> As you know, when Secretary McNamara and General Taylor came back, they announced that we would expect to withdraw 1,000 men from South Vietnam before the end of the year...If we are able to do

that, that will be our schedule. I think the first unit, the first contingent, would be 250 men who are not involved in what might be called
frontline operations. It would be our hope to lessen the number of
Americans there by 1,000 as the training intensified and is carried on
in South Vietnam...As far as other units, we will have to make that
judgment based on what the military correlation of forces may be.

He went on to laud his military build-up, which would soon permit the armed forces to deploy seven divisions quickly, a crucial
factor in the "military correlation of forces."

On the same day, a front-page story reported JFK's hopes to
withdraw 1,000 men by the end of the year as the training of
South Vietnamese is intensified. On November 13, Jack Raymond reported that Defense Officials say that the 1,000-man
withdrawal plans remain unchanged. Two days later, he reported
that at a news conference, while keeping the "official objectives
announced on October 2 to withdraw most of the troops by the
end of 1965," Kennedy weakened the withdrawal plans, reducing
the estimate for 1963 to "several hundred," pending the outcome
of the Honolulu meeting. JFK again emphasized the need to "intensify the struggle." A front-page story the next day reported
the announcement by Major-General Charles Timmes that "The
withdrawal of 1,000 United States servicemen from South Vietnam will start December 3." On November 21, the official statement from the Honolulu meeting was reported, reaffirming the
plan to withdraw 1,000 men by January 1. A December 2 item
reported General Harkins's announcement that 300 would leave
the next day. On December 4, a front-page story announced the
withdrawal of 220 GI's, the first step in withdrawal of 1,000
troops by Christmas.[65]

In short, what was public at once accurately and prominently
reflects the internal record that has now been revealed, including
some indication of JFK's personal hesitations over the withdrawal
plans recommended by his advisers.

8. The Presidential Transition

At the Honolulu meeting of November 20, a draft was prepared (signed by McGeorge Bundy) for what became NSAM 273, adopted after the assassination but intended for JFK with the expectation that he would approve it in essentials, as was the norm. Top advisers agreed; Hilsman made only "minor changes." The State Department history states that the draft "was almost identical to the final paper," differing only in paragraph 7.

NSAM 273 was declassified in May 1978; the November 20 draft, on January 31, 1991. The draft is not published in the State Department history, but its assessment is quite accurate. Both documents reiterate the basic wording of the early October documents, and call for maintaining military and economic assistance at least at previous levels. On withdrawal, the NSAM approved by Johnson is identical with the draft prepared for Kennedy. It reads: "The objectives of the United States with respect to the withdrawal of U.S. military personnel remain as stated in the White House statement of October 2, 1963," referring to the statement of US policy at the NSC meeting, formalized without essential change as NSAM 263. As for paragraph 7, the draft and final version are, respectively, as follows:

> *Draft*: With respect to action against North Vietnam, there should be a detailed plan for the development of additional Government of Vietnam resources, especially for sea-going activity, and such planning should indicate the time and investment necessary to achieve a wholly new level of effectiveness in this field of action.

> NSAM 273: Planning should include different levels of possible increased activity, and in each instance there should be estimates of such factors as:
>
> A. Resulting damage to North Vietnam;
> B. The plausibility of denial;
> C. Possible North Vietnamese retaliation;
> D. Other international reaction.

Plans should be submitted promptly for approval by higher authority.
(Action: State, DOD, and CIA)

The final phrase is attached to other paragraphs.[66]

There is no relevant difference between the two documents,
except that the LBJ version is weaker and more evasive, dropping
the call for "a wholly new level of effectiveness in this field of action"; further actions are reduced to "possible." The reason why
paragraph 7 refers to "additional" or "possible increased" activity
we have already seen: such operations had been underway since
the Kennedy offensive of 1962, apparently with direct participation of US personnel and foreign mercenaries.

As reviewed earlier, the military had advocated in January
1963 that operations against the North be continued (perhaps
intensified) as a counterpart to the plans of the hawks for withdrawal after victory, with the agreement of Hilsman and report-
edly the President. No direct US government involvement is
proposed in NSAM 273 beyond what was already underway
under JFK. Subsequent plans developed by the DOD and CIA
call for "Intensified sabotage operations in North Vietnam by
Vietnamese personnel," with the US involved only in intelligence
collection (U-2, electronics) and "psychological operations"
(leaflet drops, "phantom covert operations," "black and white
radio broadcasts").[67]

These two NSAMs (263 in October, 273 on November 26
with a November 20 draft written for Kennedy) are the center-
piece of the thesis that Kennedy planned to withdraw without
victory, a decision at once reversed by LBJ (and perhaps the
cause of the assassination). They have been the subject of many
claims and charges. Typical of the 1992 revival is Oliver Stone's
address to the National Press Club alleging that John Newman's
study "makes it very clear President Kennedy signaled his intention to withdraw from Vietnam in a variety of ways and put that

intention firmly on the record with National Security Action Memorandum 263 in October of 1963," while LBJ "reverse[d] the NSAM" with NSAM 273. Arthur Schlesinger claimed that after the assassination, "President Johnson, listening to President Kennedy's more hawkish advisers and believing that he was doing what President Kennedy would have done, issued National Security Action Memorandum 273 calling for the maintenance of American military programs in Vietnam 'at levels as high' as before—reversing the Kennedy withdrawal policy." The co-author (with Stone) of the screenplay *JFK*, Zachary Sklar, also citing Newman's book, claims further that the draft prepared for Kennedy "says that the U.S. will *train the South Vietnamese* to carry out covert military operations against North Vietnam" while "In the final document, signed by Johnson, it states that *U.S. forces* themselves will carry out these covert military operations," leading to the Tonkin Gulf incident, which "was an example of precisely that kind of covert operation carried out by U.S. forces" (his emphasis).[68]

Such claims, which are common, are groundless, indeed are refuted by the internal record. Newman's book adds nothing relevant to the available record, which gives no hint of any intention by JFK to withdraw without victory—quite the contrary—and reveals no "reversal" in NSAM 273. The call for maintenance of aid is in the draft of NSAM 273 prepared for Kennedy, and was also at the core of his tentative withdrawal plans, conditioned on victory and "Major U.S. assistance" to assure it. Furthermore, Kennedy's *more dovish*—not "more hawkish"—advisers approved and continued to urge LBJ to follow what they understood to be JFK's policy, rejecting any thought of withdrawal without victory. The final version of NSAM 273 does not state that US forces would carry out covert operations in any new way; nor did they, in the following months. There were covert attacks on North Vietnamese installations just prior to the Tonkin Gulf incident, but they were carried out by South Vietnamese forces, according to the internal record.

The two versions of NSAM 273 differ in no relevant way, apart from the weakening of paragraph 7 in the final version. Furthermore, the departure from NSAM 263 is slight, and readily explained in terms of changing assessments. Efforts to detect nuances and hidden implications have no basis in fact, and if pursued, could easily be turned into a (meaningless) "proof" that LBJ toned down Kennedy aggressiveness.

The call in paragraph 7 for consideration of further ARVN operations against the North is readily explained in terms of the two basic features of the post-coup situation: the feeling among Kennedy's war planners that with the Diem regime gone, the US at last had a regime committed to Kennedy's war in the South, offering new "opportunities to exploit"; and the increasing concern about the military situation in the South, undermining earlier optimism. The former factor made it possible to consider extension of ARVN operations; the latter made it more important to extend them. In subsequent months, Kennedy's planners (now directing Johnson's war) increasingly inclined towards operations against the North as a way to overcome their inability to win the war in the South, leading finally to the escalation of 1965, undertaken largely to "drive the DRV out of its reinforcing role and obtain its cooperation in bringing an end to the Viet Cong insurgency," using "its directive powers to make the Viet Cong desist" (Taylor, November 27, 1964).[69]

9. LBJ and the Kennedy Doves

Kennedy's more dovish advisers recommended the policies that Johnson pursued, and generally approved of them until the 1965 escalation, often beyond. They lost no time in making clear that JFK's commitment to victory would not be abandoned. On December 10, Forrestal, Ball, Harriman, and Hilsman, reiterating JFK's consistent stand, assured Lodge that "we are against neutralism and want to win the war." The same unwavering commitment was reiterated by George Ball, perhaps the most consistent dove among them. On December 16, he informed Lodge that "Nothing is further from USG mind than 'neutral solution for Vietnam.' We intend to win." A year later (November 1964), having returned to a more active role in Vietnam planning, Ball held that the Saigon regime must continue to receive US aid until the Viet Cong is defeated and agreed that "the struggle would be a long one, even with the DRV out of it." In July 1965, he advised LBJ that "Securing the Mekong Valley will be critical in any long-run solution, whether by the partition of Laos with Thai-U.S. forces occupying the western half or by some cover arrangement." These recommendations illustrate what "dove" meant in Camelot.[70]

Ball and other JFK doves continued to support Johnson's policies, which they regarded as a continuation of Kennedy's. Writing to the Secretary of State on May 31, 1964, Ball praised "the President's wise caution" and refusal to "act hastily." Against that background, Ball added, he and Alexis Johnson had "considerably slowed down the headlong crystallization of a plan for enlarging the war" developed by other advisers, including some considered doves.[71]

Ball's later reflections on Kennedy's attitudes are also worth noting. He writes that he had "strongly opposed" Kennedy's November 1961 decision to commit US forces to South Vietnam, predicting to him that it would drag the US into a morass with "three hundred thousand men in the paddies and jungles." These pessimistic predictions "were not words the President wanted to hear," and he responded "with an overtone of asperity" in terms that Ball says he never quite understood. "Kennedy's reaction deterred me from expressing opposition to the war until after the Tonkin Gulf incident" in August 1964, Ball adds. Ball notes that had he lived, "Kennedy would almost certainly have received the same advice and pressures from the same group of advisers who persuaded Johnson to deepen America's involvement." He has no clear opinion as to how JFK would have reacted. Noting further that "some historians have adduced bits of evidence to show that President Kennedy had reserved in his own mind the possibility of withdrawal," Ball writes that he can "venture no opinion." Note that the most he contemplates is that JFK might have had the *possibility* in mind.[72]

In his attempt to show that JFK favored withdrawal, John Newman claims that Ball, who replaced the more dovish Chester Bowles as Under Secretary of State in November 1961, "was acceptable to Kennedy because he too opposed sending U.S. combat troops to Vietnam"—as doubtless he did, along with much of the top military. But Newman's unsupported judgment about Kennedy's reasons does not quite square with Ball's own.[73]

Bowles became Ambassador at Large, then Ambassador to India. Like John Kenneth Galbraith and others who favored political settlement over military victory, he was distanced from policy planning by Kennedy, and scarcely appears in the internal record. There was no place for such views in JFK's Vietnam programs.

Senate Majority Leader Mike Mansfield is another interesting case. A regular participant in high-level meetings with a special interest in Asian affairs, he is depicted in much later commentary as an advocate of withdrawal to whom Kennedy confided his secret plans; for Schlesinger and Newman, this claim takes on central importance, as we shall see. Neither the internal nor public record treats it kindly.

Like other influential Senators, Mansfield had been concerned over the consequences of Kennedy's war. His objections, however, were tactical and qualified. There was no real US interest at stake that would justify spending "countless American lives and billions of dollars to maintain an illusion of freedom in a devastated South

Viet Nam," he felt. It would be dangerous to find ourselves
"bogged down" in a region that is "peripheral to [US] interests,"
he advised JFK in August 1963. Mansfield therefore suggested that
"rhetorical flourishes" be abandoned and that "We should stress
not the vague 'vital importance' of the area to the U.S.," but its
"relatively limited importance"; and that as a warning to Diem, who
was not fighting the war successfully, some 1,500 military advisers
should be withdrawn "as a symbolic gesture, to make clear that we
mean business when we say that there are some circumstances in
which this commitment will be discontinued." The first of these
proposals JFK flatly rejected; as we have seen, to the end he
stressed the "vital importance" of victory. Whether he accepted the
second is a matter of interpretation of hidden intentions: if so, it is
hardly comforting to the withdrawal thesis.

After the assassination, Mansfield advised LBJ to seek a general truce "at a price commensurate with American interests."
He recommended "an effort to strengthen the hold of the Saigon
government on those parts of South Viet Nam which it now controls," instead of a hopeless "chase of the Viet Cong all over the
land." Mansfield was particularly satisfied by Lyndon Johnson's
continuation of Kennedy's policies. At a meeting of the National
Security Council on April 3, 1964, LBJ rejected Senator Morse's
proposal for "using SEATO and the UN to achieve a peaceful
settlement," informing him that the Administration accepted
McNamara's views that withdrawal or neutralization would lead
to a Communist takeover and therefore remain unacceptable options. Mansfield approved, urging "that the President's policy toward Vietnam was the only one we could follow." He firmly
rejected the withdrawal option and the diplomatic moves coun-
selled by Morse.

Mansfield continued to have tactical reservations, however.
In December 1964 he advised LBJ "that American and Western
interests are best served by the frugal use of American resources

to forestall Chinese political and military domination of the area," and opposed "a vast increase in the commitment." Commenting on Mansfield's position, McGeorge Bundy informed the President that there was only "a difference in emphasis between him and us, but certainly no difference in fundamental purpose." That seems accurate. A few weeks later (January 3, 1965), Mansfield publicly supported "the President's desire neither to withdraw nor carry the war to North Vietnam," the *Pentagon Papers* analyst observes. Once the bombing of the North began and a huge US expeditionary force was deployed, Mansfield demanded obedience. When the first major protest against the bombing of the North took place in October 1965, he condemned "the sense of utter irresponsibility" of those who dared question the violence of the state.[74]

Mansfield's reaction was hardly unusual. To cite another prominent example, House Speaker Thomas (Tip) O'Neil of Massachusetts, later portrayed as a strong opponent of the war, refused in April 1965 to allow a delegation of university professors from his constituency even to enter his office to raise questions about his leader's war policies.

JFK's top advisers (McNamara, Bundy, Rusk) advised LBJ in January 1964 to reject Mansfield's recommendations and to keep to Kennedy's more militant policies. McNamara held that any sign of hesitation by the US *"would inevitably mean a new government in Saigon that would in short order become Communist-dominated,"* with consequences for the US position in Asia "and indeed in other key areas of the world" that *"are extremely serious"*; the stakes are "so high" that "we must go on bending every effort to win." Kennedy's close associate Theodore Sorenson, still on the White House staff, agreed "that the partition or neutralization of South Vietnam today, or even our proposing such partition or neutralization, would, *under present conditions*, lead to a Communist takeover in that country, a weakening of our prestige and security throughout

Asia and an increase in the possibilities of a major military involvement in that area." The only merit Sorenson saw in a proposal for neutralization of all of Vietnam or a cease-fire would be that rejection by the Communists would facilitate the US war effort. He also urged that LBJ reiterate the standard theme that it is up to the South Vietnamese to win the war, so that the onus will be on them, not us, if things fall apart.[75]

In brief, Kennedy's top advisers, including the most dovish among them, sensed no change at the transition and lent their support to Johnson. Some praised his "wise caution," while others, as we see directly, called for more aggressive action. That reaction is natural, given their familiarity with the internal record, which shows no deviation on JFK's part from Harriman's judgment "there are no quitters here."

Of course, in thousands of pages of documents one can find occasional variation in wording and nuance. Furthermore, this is history, not quantum physics: judgments must always be qualified. But such reservations aside, the internal record largely confirms what was made public in the fall of 1963 on the issue of withdrawal, and portrays JFK only as less willing than his top advisers to commit himself to withdrawal—and surely not without victory. Furthermore, the consistency of the record in this regard, from every perspective, is quite striking.

10. "A Hostile Territory"

Continuing with the internal record into the Johnson Administration, on November 27 Hilsman informed a representative of the Saigon government that the withdrawal plans remained in force though "we shall keep in Viet-Nam whatever forces are needed for victory." On December 2, General Harkins announced withdrawal of 300 military personnel the next day and another 700 in the following weeks, "making a total reduction in force of 1000 before the end of 1963" (reported in the press, as noted).

An internal DOD memorandum of March 2, 1964, states that "In December 1000 men came home," including "two military police units whose airport guard duty had been taken over by Vietnamese trained for that purpose." It called for continued training missions so that US troops can be withdrawn. The details of what happened are murky. But the question is academic, in light of radically revised assessments of the military situation, which canceled the assumptions on which the withdrawal plans had been conditioned.

The first report prepared for LBJ (November 23) opened with this *"Summary Assessment"*: "The outlook is hopeful. There is better assurance than under Diem that the war can be won. We are pulling out 1,000 American troops by the end of 1963." Apart from a serious budgetary deficit, the "main concern is whether the generals can hold together until victory has been achieved." The next day, however, CIA Director John McCone informed the President that the CIA now regarded the situation as "somewhat more serious" than had been thought, with "a continuing increase in Viet Cong activity since the first of November" (the coup). Subsequent reports only deepened the gloom.[76]

On December 6, the CIA reported that VC activity had increased since mid-1963, "reaching record peaks since the coup" and becoming "more effective." The DOD confirmed this "disturbing analysis of the current military situation," urging pressures against North Vietnam. Estimates of past success were sharply reduced. Forrestal informed the President that recent reports were "rather alarming," though the ruling generals offered better prospects than the Diem regime. Previous reports had been "too optimistic." Pentagon Intelligence (DIA) informed McNamara that "The Viet Cong by and large retain de facto control of much of the countryside and have steadily increased the overall intensity of the effort" since February 1963, reaching an "all-time high" in "incidents and armed attacks" after the No-

vember 1 coup. Though "only 914 persons are known to have
been introduced into the RVN during 1963" and there were an
estimated 27,000 VC casualties in 1963 through November, VC
force levels remained stable, indicating that casualties were being
replaced "through extensive local recruitment." The CIA added
that "the VC have made definite progress," with the Strategic
Hamlet Program "particularly hard hit in certain provinces." The
CIA was unsure whether the problems "are only now coming to
light under the country's new management, or whether it is the
result of the current lack of firm leadership at the local and national levels" (December 16). In critical Long An province near
Saigon, barely more than 10 percent of the Hamlets "previously
reported as completed" were actually functional. By December
21, General Krulak, previously an optimist, warned the Joint
Chiefs of the seriousness of the situation, judging the government's position to be "much weaker now than two to six months
ago," when the withdrawal option seemed feasible to them.[77]

Krulak was reporting on a December 19-20 McNamara visit
to Saigon. Under Secretary of State William Sullivan added that
reports by US military and province advisers "were uniformly dis-
couraging and indicated a considerable falsification of data by the
previous Vietnamese regime." "The visit was a sobering one," he
added. Reporting to the President, McNamara described the situation as "very disturbing": "Current trends, unless reversed in the
next 2-3 months, will lead to neutralization at best and more likely
to a Communist-controlled state." The situation had been "deteriorating in the countryside since July to a for greater extent than
we realized" and Viet Cong progress since the coup "has been
great." In light of this sharply changed assessment, McNamara
said nothing about withdrawal, recommending only that "U.S. resources and personnel cannot usefully be substantially increased,"
though we should be "preparing for more forceful moves if the situation does not show early signs of improvement" (his emphasis).

McCone agreed that "indices on progress of the war turned
unfavorable for the GVN" about July 1963, moving "very sharply
against the GVN" after the coup. He reported an estimate of
1,550 infiltrators from North Vietnam for 1963 (roughly the
same as McNamara); MACV estimated "more than 7600" since
January 1961, declining to about 1,000 in 1963, mostly "political
cadres," adding that "external supply of arms is not a critical matter." The worst problem, McCone reported, is that "The VC appeal to the people of South Vietnam on political grounds has
been effective," something that the US could never counter. Sullivan reported that "There is a People's Republic of the Viet
Cong" running from Saigon through most of the Delta, "a well-
established subsisting entity which probably pays its own way,
even with regard to the war material which it imports from the
outside world." GVN Commander-in-Chief General Don said
that "We are like an expeditionary force in a hostile territory,
holding only a few strong points and maintaining only a few main
roads of communication." "The abrupt exposure of the true situation that had developed throughout the country came as a surprise and shock to many Vietnamese and Americans," another
State Department official reported on December 31.[78]

11. Going North

Continuing into 1964, we find the same pattern of planning and
debate as under Kennedy, modified only in that the 1962-1963
optimism about imminent victory is abandoned, as the truth
about the military situation finally penetrated and the US failed
to impose a government that would unleash the requisite resources of "great violence" and control its population with Hitler-
style efficiency, thus overcoming the defects that dismayed
Lodge. As the year opened, Lodge reported to LBJ that while
the overthrow of Diem prevented "certain catastrophe," we are
"now just beginning to see the full extent of the dry rot and las-

situde in the Government of Viet-Nam and the extent to which we were given inaccurate information" (January 1). McCone reported that the military field officers "had been grossly misinformed" by their Vietnamese associates, urging that US intelligence bypass them henceforth and make its own assessments (January 7). McNamara and others also learned more about the "grossly inaccurate picture" on which they had been basing their plans (Forrestal, January 8).[79]

A few weeks later, the Joint Chiefs recommended that the US "Induce the Government of Vietnam to conduct overt ground operations in Laos of sufficient scope to impede the flow of personnel and material southward," and "Arm, equip, advise and support the Government of Vietnam in its conduct of aerial bombing of critical targets in North Vietnam and in mining the sea approaches to that country." They recommended further that the US itself "Conduct aerial bombing of key North Vietnam targets," "Commit additional US forces, as necessary, in support of the combat action within South Vietnam," and "Commit US forces as necessary in direct actions against North Vietnam" (Taylor, January 22).[80]

McNamara's DOD rejected this advice, proposing only to "continue our present policy of providing training and logistical support for the South Vietnam forces," without direct US involvement (March 2). LBJ uneasily dragged his feet. In a meeting with the Joint Chiefs on March 4, he made it clear "that he does not want to lose South Vietnam before next November nor does he want to get the country into war" (Taylor Memorandum). On March 17, he rejected the JCS request for "putting in more U.S. forces" and refused to authorize even "reconnaissance over North Vietnam."[81]

By then, some of the Kennedy doves were tending towards escalation. Forrestal observed on March 18 that "I am somewhat more worried by those who argue for a bug out in Southeast Asia

than I am by the adherents of Rostow," the superhawk; that these
were the alternatives was becoming the consensus view. As the
US position in the South deteriorated, Forrestal increasingly favored escalation of actions against the North along with an intensified counterinsurgency program, later supporting the Joint
Chiefs on air and ground operations in Laos as well.[82]

Hilsman's position was similar. On leaving the government,
he wrote a secret memorandum (March 14) in which he emphasized the need to assure Asians, friend or enemy, of "U.S. determination to use appropriate force, tailored to the essentially
limited political objectives...." We must show that "we are determined to take whatever measures are necessary in Southeast Asia
to protect those who oppose the Communists and to maintain our
power and influence in the area," and therefore "must urgently
begin to strengthen our overall military posture in Southeast Asia
in ways which will make it clear that we are single-mindedly improving our capability to take whatever military steps may be necessary to halt Communist aggression in the area" (crucially, Viet
Cong "aggression"). We might station a Marine battalion in
Saigon on the pretext of protecting American dependents. Attacks
against the North might be "a useful *supplement* to an effective
counterinsurgency program," but not "an effective *substitute*" for
it. We must "continue the covert, or at least deniable, operations"
against the North in order to keep "the threat of eventual destruction alive in Hanoi's mind."[83]

Recall that Hilsman had made the same recommendations
in April 1963, in virtually the same words, including the advice
to "continue" the ongoing covert operations against the North
with their implicit threat of destruction; that he had advised the
deployment of US combat forces to assist the rebel generals in
the event of any hint that Diem and Nhu were seeking a political
settlement, and the use of unlimited force against the DRV if
they sought "to counter our actions"; and that after the assassi-

nation, he had assured the GVN that "we shall keep in Viet-Nam whatever forces are needed for victory."

By March 30, "all the Chiefs except General Taylor wanted to go north," the White House was informed. Forrestal supported the Chiefs' call for "overt SVN action with U.S. covert support," but wanted "direct U.S. action as a contingency," for the moment. LBJ continued to reject either withdrawal or escalation. Mansfield approved, as noted. We must "help the Vietnamese to help themselves," LBJ informed Lodge, nothing more (April 28).[84]

In late May, McGeorge Bundy advised "selected and carefully graduated military force against North Vietnam," while Forrestal, after a two-week visit to South Vietnam, reported his "very strong personal opinion" that "the United States must take a fairly dramatic step soon against the North," along with an eventual "increase both in the American military and civilian presence in the countryside" in the South. On June 2, the Joint Chiefs again called for "military actions to accomplish destruction of the North Vietnamese will and capabilities as necessary to compel [the DRV] to cease providing support" for insurgent activities in Laos and Vietnam. LBJ continued to hold back. When two US reconnaissance planes were shot down in Laos, he approved a retaliatory attack on an antiaircraft installation only "with grave reservations."

On August 2, the US destroyer *Maddox* was attacked in Tonkin Gulf. Forrestal urged that US naval units should operate within the 12-mile limit "probably" claimed by North Vietnam and suggested that thought be given to "hot pursuit" to a distance of three miles as well as aerial mining of harbors and "an unidentified air strike against one or more of these harbors." He recognized at once that "the North Vietnamese and perhaps the Chicoms" had probably taken the *Maddox* to be accompanying the "OPLAN 34A harassing action by SVN forces against two islands off the DRV coast" at the same time. CIA Director McCone informed the National Security Council that "The North Vietnamese are reacting

defensively to our attacks on their off-shore islands." The State Department assumed the same, as it issued a strong public condemnation of the "unprovoked attack," and the Administration drafted
the congressional resolution denouncing "unprovoked armed attacks" that was later used as the justification for escalation.[85]

By late August, JCS appeals for direct US military involvement became more strident. They advised McNamara that "accelerated and forceful action with respect to North Vietnam is
essential to prevent a complete collapse of the US position in
Southeast Asia." Bundy informed the President that "landing a
limited number of Marines to guard specific installations" was
under discussion, though McNamara was "very strongly against"
that course. Bundy thought that "before we let this country go
we should have a hard look" at the "grim alternative" of using
"substantial U.S. armed forces" (August 31).[86]

Note that this is almost a year after the assassination, which,
it is alleged, gave the hawks free rein to take over and escalate
the war (or even was perpetrated by them to place their man, the
hawkish LBJ, in power).

With intelligence reporting (September 8) that "the present
situation is far more serious than that of November 1963," the
consensus of the President's advisers was that it would be necessary to resume US naval patrols and "34A operations by the
GVN," along with "limited GVN air and ground operations" in
southern Laos, though only after a stable base was established
in South Vietnam. LBJ agreed, opposing "those advocating immediate and extensive action against the North." NSAM 314
(September 10) approved US naval patrols "well beyond [out-
side] the 12-mile limit" and "clearly dissociated from 34A mar-
itime operations" by the GVN, with no GVN air strikes
considered for the present, and an emphasis on "economic and
political actions," at LBJ's insistence. After another alleged Gulf
of Tonkin incident a week later, the President was "very skeptical

about the evidence" and rejected the advice for "rapid escalation," indeed any response. He "again found [considerable]
force" in George Ball's qualms about conducting naval patrols at
all, again lining up with the more extreme Kennedy doves.

On October 1, intelligence reported further deterioration in
South Vietnam, and the JCS reiterated their demand for "strong
military actions...to prevent the collapse of the US position in
Southeast Asia" (October 27). Taylor, who had replaced Lodge
as Ambassador, continued to oppose the use of US forces (see
below). On November 23, the Chiefs advised a "controlled program of intense military pressures against the DRV." Taylor informed Washington that "the northern provinces of South
Viet-Nam which a year ago were considered almost free of Viet-
Cong are now in deep trouble," and only "heroic treatment"
could revive the counterinsurgency program, which is "bogged
down" everywhere. No options remain except compelling the
DRV to "make the Viet-Cong desist." After an unattributed
bombing in the South, Taylor and the military command recommended "forty strike sorties" against the DRV in "retaliation,"
which would "do wonders for the morale of U.S. personnel in
South Vietnam," McGeorge Bundy urged the President (December 28). The President rejected these proposals, proposing instead that Rangers, Special Forces, and Marines might be used
"to stiffen the aggressiveness of Vietnamese military units."[87]

So 1964 ends, and with it, the extensive record of newly-
released documents. Their contribution is to undermine much
further the already implausible contention that JFK intended
to withdraw without victory and that the assassination caused
dramatic changes in policy (or, indeed, had any effect). Just as
there is no hint in the record of any such intention on JFK's
part, there is also no indication that his advisers, however
dovish, felt that President Johnson was urging too aggressive a
course or had departed from JFK's stand. On the contrary,

Johnson remained skeptical and reluctant about US military action throughout, earning the applause of Ball and Mansfield for
his "wise caution," while other JFK doves urged stronger US
military actions. The belief that JFK might have responded differently as the optimistic projections of 1962-1963 collapsed is
an act of faith, based on nothing but the belief that the President had some spiritual quality absent in everyone around him,
leaving no detectable trace.

12. Militarily Strong, Politically Weak

The basic problem that McCone had stressed in December 1963
was well understood. The VC "believe in something," Lodge reported in January 1964: "the Communists have conveyed to these
men [a] clear picture of a program which they think will make life
better. We have not. They are also well organized politically; we
are not." The US client regime has overwhelming military advan-
tages, but "the VC have simply shifted from military to political
tactics and are defeating us politically," following "the old Mao
Tse-tung maxim." "We are at present overwhelmingly outclassed
politically." We must "enunciate a political program" and organize
precinct workers. The US is militarily strong but politically weak,
unable to enlist support for its plans for the Third World, a persistent problem in Indochina as elsewhere, always a mystery to
the planners.

US disadvantages were compounded by a problem discov-
ered by Hubert Humphrey on a June visit: "the relatively indiscriminate use of heavy weapons and napalm are not calculated
to win the support of the people," he found. Furthermore, "A
political base is needed to support all other actions toward gaining victory," and we should guide the Vietnamese to develop such
a base, which the Vietnamese, unlike the Viet Cong, sorely lack.
He too rejected any thought of withdrawal without victory or
permitting "a 'neutralist' solution," which would signal "to the

people of southeast Asia that we have lost confidence in them and that the game is lost." "The people" are our favorite generals, for this shining light of American liberalism.[88]

In November 1964, Ambassador Taylor wrote a think-piece on these political problems, revealing the astuteness that caught the eye of JFK, whom he had impressed as "an intellectual who quoted Thucydides" as well as an expert in "unconventional warfare," Newman writes (127, citing David Halberstam). Taylor deplored the "national attribute which makes for factionalism and limits the development of a truly national spirit" among the Vietnamese, perhaps "innate" or a result of their history of "political suppression" under the French. This "national attribute" makes it difficult for the Vietnamese to confront the Viet Cong, who "have an amazing ability to maintain morale" and are able "continuously to rebuild their units and to make good their losses," exhibiting "the recuperative powers of the phoenix." This is "one of the mysteries of this guerrilla war," JFK's specialist on political warfare lamented, adding that "we still find no plausible explanation" for it. Since "we are playing a losing game in South Viet-Nam" (the political game), "it is high time we change and find a better way": pressuring the DRV to direct an end to the southern resistance.[89] Only North Vietnamese orders can now compel the VC aggressors, who are so radically different from the Vietnamese in their innate and acquired characteristics, to end their "assault from the inside" (JFK) and to dismantle the political base that we cannot duplicate.

Such thoughts appear throughout the internal record, as in public commentary. For the planners, as for the political class generally, it is never easy to comprehend why backward peoples to whom we minister do not comprehend our magnificence, why "their side" looks ten-feet tall while "our side" are crooks and gangsters, suffering from defects that may even be "innate." And in contemplating these mysteries, they easily fall into musings, even self-contradiction, that would be comical if the conse-

quences for the victims were not so disastrous. These are enduring themes of the 500-year conquest, sure to persist.

13. The Military View

One might ask why the military command failed to recognize the
truth about the situation in the countryside. The matter is addressed by the military historian on whom Newman heavily relies, Andrew Krepinich, who explains that the top command was
guided by a "Concept" drawn from World War II doctrine, which
was challenged by negative reports from the field; these were accordingly disregarded, a fact that will surprise no one familiar
with military history—or Tolstoy's novels.[90]

After the Diem assassination (which the military opposed,
predicting accurately that it would cause the military situation to
deteriorate), the bureaucratic structure eroded and the truth
began to filter through, leading to revision of planning. But false
reports from the military command continued to mislead the top
civilian leadership up to the 1968 Tet Offensive. One close associate of Johnson's, who sat in on the highest-level planning meetings in those years and was also briefed regularly by field-grade
officers and CIA personnel, informed me privately that pessimistic reports from the field were regularly transmuted to encouraging signs of progress as they reached the President's
highest advisers, through the natural process by which subordi-
nates tailor their reports to what they know is preferred, and people hear what they want to hear.

As is often the case, the top military leadership were sharply
divided over the war. In April 1961, General Douglas MacArthur
warned JFK that it would be a "mistake" to fight in Southeast
Asia altogether, and that "our line should be Japan, Formosa and
the Philippines." The same stand was taken by MacArthur's successor as Army Chief of Staff, General Matthew Ridgway, who
"argued in a continuous barrage of memoranda that the United

States should steer clear of an Asian land war," Marcus Raskin notes. Ridgway had strongly opposed US intervention in 1954. Even a limited US presence in Southeast Asia "had an ominous ring," he wrote in 1956, for it would inevitably lead to a commitment of ground forces. On US air support, Ridgway recalled Korea, finding it "incredible...that we were on the verge of making that same tragic error," as Kennedy did shortly after. Later too he "passionately opposed intervention in Vietnam," military historian Robert Buzzanco writes. Army Plans Chief General James Gavin also warned against US intervention, and continued to criticize US involvement in Indochina through the Eisenhower years, later advocating the "enclave strategy." In a 1954 planning study commissioned by Ridgway, Gavin found that intervention would require vast military resources. He also warned against the effect of interservice rivalries in driving policy, noting in the late 1950s that "What appears to be intense interservice rivalry in most cases...is fundamentally industrial rivalry." General J. Lawton Collins was another critic of intervention, saying later that he did not "know of a single senior commander that was in favor of fighting on the land mass of Asia."

"Indeed, more than any other institution—in or outside of government—the U.S. armed forces worked against military involvement in the first Indochina war," Buzzanco concludes, from July 1949, when the Chiefs warned that the "widening political consciousness and the rise of militant nationalism among the subject people" could not be crushed by force and that Vietnamese nationalism "cannot be reversed." The Chiefs were "unanimously opposed to the commitment of any troops," Defense Secretary Robert Lovett wrote NATO Commander Eisenhower in 1952. The NSC civilian leadership, in contrast, favored a troop commitment. The JCS "insisted that the United States must not be committed financially, militarily, or economically" to intervention in Southeast Asia, the *Pentagon Papers* analyst concluded. A 1954

JCS report concluded that "no amount of external pressure and
assistance can long delay complete Communist victory in South
Vietnam," without a strong base of popular support. Army planners had estimated in 1950 that 80 percent of Vietnamese supported Ho Chi Minh, and of those, 80 percent were not
Communists, an assessment that did not change. US government
studies of VC defectors and prisoners 15 years later found that
"few of them considered themselves Communists or could give a
definition of Communism," or were aware of any North Vietnamese role in the war "except as a valued ally."[91]

Despite the changes introduced by Kennedy's "action intellectuals," these attitudes did not disappear. The top US military
commander in Vietnam, MAAG Chief General Lionel McGarr,
informed JFK on February 22, 1962 that "in providing the GVN
the tools to do the job," the US "must not offer so much that they
forget that the job of saving the country is theirs—only they can
do it." Robert Buzzanco, who has given the closest scholarly attention to this topic, concludes that "notwithstanding John Newman's recent argument that the JCS pressured President John F.
Kennedy into deeper commitments to the RVN despite his grave
reservations, there is ample evidence that even in the early 1960s
the military did not feel compelled to intervene in Indochina."[92]

Kennedy's most trusted military adviser, General Taylor,
shared the doubts of other senior commanders about dispatch of
combat troops, as did Pacific Commander Admiral Henry Felt.
As plans to overthrow the Diem-Nhu regime were underway in
September 1963, Taylor expressed his "reluctance to contemplate
the use of U.S. troops in combat in Vietnam," while agreeing with
the President and his other top advisers that "our sole objective
was to win the war." A year after the assassination, in September
1964, Taylor explained that MACV "did not contemplate" committing combat forces because Commanding General Westmoreland, echoing McGarr, felt that the use of American troops

"would be a mistake, that it is the Vietnamese' war." Agreeing, Taylor continued to urge that the US keep to the "principle that the Vietnamese fight their own war in SVN" (November 3, 1964). He therefore opposed sending logistical forces for flood relief because that would require dispatch of "US combat troops in some numbers to provide close protection." He argued that the situation was not comparable to the far more severe 1961 flood, when he had recommended dispatch of "US logistic units with combat support" for "flood relief operations." Two weeks later, he informed President Johnson that he was now "quite certain [US combat troops] were not needed...as the estimates of the flood damage diminish." His objection to sending combat forces continued. In February 1965, he opposed General Westmoreland's request for Marines to protect the US air base at Danang, arguing again that it would be "very difficult to hold the line on future deployments" and that the US should keep to the "long standing policies of avoiding commitment of ground combat forces in South Vietnam." When his advice was rejected, he advocated the "enclave strategy" proposed by the extreme doves.[93]

In later years, as we shall see, great import has been attributed to JFK's public reiteration of the McGarr-Westmoreland-Taylor "principle" in his September 1963 statement that "In the final analysis it is their war. They have to win it or lose it." It is, therefore, worth stressing that the "principle" was standard throughout in internal and public discussion. The McNamara-Taylor report to the President of October 2 stated that "The U.S. advisory effort, however, cannot assure ultimate success. This is a Vietnamese war and the country and the war must, in the end, be run solely by the Vietnamese. It will impair their independence and development of their initiative if we leave our advisers in place beyond the time they are really needed...." High-ranking officials kept to that position as long as there appeared to be hopes for victory in these terms. In testimony before the House

Armed Services Committee in late January 1964, McNamara stated that "It is a Vietnamese war. They are going to have to assume the primary responsibility for winning it. Our policy is to limit our support to logistical and training support... Our responsibility is not to substitute ourselves for the Vietnamese, but to train them to carry on the operations that they themselves are capable of" in this "counterguerrilla war," which "can only be won by the Vietnamese themselves." He reiterated his expectation that withdrawal could proceed as planned.[94]

Later, as the premises concerning victory were seen to be unrealistic, McNamara and others changed their tactical stance. It is, again, merely an act of faith to assume that JFK's reaction to changed assessments would have differed from that of his most trusted advisers, to whom he had delegated responsibility for the war.

Taylor also "strongly opposed" the decision to request combat troops in March 1965 as the Saigon military was on the verge of collapse, and continued to oppose the "hasty and ill-conceived" proposals for a greater commitment. Bergerud notes that in mid-1965, "Ambassador Maxwell Taylor and George Ball argued for sharply limited American force levels and the employment of U.S. troops in and around strategic 'enclaves'." Taylor's "principle that the Vietnamese fight their own war" was, however, a matter of tactical judgment, based on an assessment that there would be "no clear gain" in a departure from it (November 3, 1964). In this respect, he was at one with JFK, so the available record indicates.

Speaking to fellow officers in 1963, incoming Marine Commandant Wallace Greene warned that US troops were "mired down in South Vietnam...and we don't seem to be able to do much about it." The Marines "do not want to get any more involved in South Vietnam," he informed them. A March 1964 report by MACV planner General Richard Stillwell confirmed Greene's judgment, recommending various actions but not US combat troops.

In January 1965, the MACV staff, with Taylor's concurrence, continued to oppose US combat troops, which "would at best buy time and would lead to ever increasing commitments until, like the French, we would be occupying an essentially hostile foreign country." In May 1965, Greene warned again that this "unwanted, undesired, miserable war" was getting worse, noting that at least half the US population "don't want anything to do with it."

Greene's predecessor General David Shoup, Marine Commandant through the Kennedy years and known as Kennedy's "favorite service chief," reports that when the Joint Chiefs considered troop deployment, "in every case...every senior officer that I knew...said we should never send ground combat forces into Southeast Asia." Shoup was a particularly strong opponent of the war. It would be hard to find a civilian figure who came close to the views he expressed in a May 1966 speech at Junior College World Affairs Day:

> I believe that if we had and would keep our dirty, bloody, dollar-crooked fingers out of the business of these nations so full of depressed, exploited people, they will arrive at a solution of their own. That they design and want. That they fight and work for. [Not one] crammed down their throats by Americans.

Surely Arthur Schlesinger and others who later described themselves as opponents of escalation took no such stand; nor did media doves.[95]

These observations add further weight to the conclusion based on the record of internal deliberations, in which JFK insists upon victory and considers withdrawal only on this condition. Had he intended to withdraw, he would have been able to enlist respected military commanders to back him. He made no effort to do so, preferring instead to whip up pro-war sentiment by extravagant rhetoric about the enormous stakes that require us to stand firm, come what may.

2

Interpretations

We have reviewed the first three categories of evidence concerning Kennedy's war and plans, and the presidential transition: the events themselves, public statements, and the internal record. The last source of evidence is the memoirs and other comments of his associates. These come in two versions: before and after the Tet Offensive. We review these in the next two sections, then turning to the 1991-1992 revival. This survey only adds conviction to what we have already found, while shedding interesting light on the cultural scene.

1. The Early Version

Kennedy's commitment to stay the course was clear to those closest to him. As noted, Arthur Schlesinger shared JFK's perception of the enormous stakes and his optimism that the military escalation had reversed the "aggression" of the indigenous guerrillas in 1962. There is not a word in Schlesinger's chronicle of the Kennedy years that hints of any intention, however vague, to withdraw without victory (1965, reprinted 1967).

In fact, Schlesinger gives no indication that JFK thought about withdrawal at all. The withdrawal plans receive one sentence in his voluminous text. In the context of the debate over pressuring the Diem regime, Schlesinger writes that McNamara returned from Saigon in October 1963 and

131

"announced...that a thousand American troops could be withdrawn by the end of the year and that the major part of the
American military task would be completed by the end of
1965." That is the entire discussion of withdrawal plans in this
940-page virtual day-by-day record of the Kennedy Administration by its quasi-official historian.[1]

These facts leave only three possible conclusions: (1) the historian was keeping the President's intentions secret; (2) this close
JFK confidant had no inkling of his intentions; (3) there were no
such intentions.

Which is it? The question is addressed only obliquely by advocates of the withdrawal-without-victory thesis. The only plausible conclusion is (3), but that is rejected by the advocates,
leaving (1) or (2). The latter might strain credulity, unless taken
to show the lengths to which JFK went to deceive all around him.
Newman cites Schlesinger's justification in 1978 of JFK's "decision to hide his plans" (324), implying that the correct conclusion
is (1)—unless Schlesinger had learned about these "secret plans"
in the interim, which no one claims, including Schlesinger himself. Hence Schlesinger too must be adopting (1). Furthermore,
he lauds Newman's book with no relevant reservations, again
suggesting that he regards (1) as accurate. One would be interested to hear an explanation.

Similar questions arise in the case of another close associate,
Theodore Sorenson, who also published a history of the Administration in 1965. Sorenson was Kennedy's first appointed official, served as his special counsel, and attended all NSC
meetings. He stayed on through the early months of the Johnson Administration. He devotes little attention to Vietnam. No
withdrawal plans are mentioned. Quite the contrary. Kennedy's
"essential contribution" was to avoid the extremes advocated "by
those impatient to win or withdraw. His strategy essentially was
to avoid escalation, retreat or a choice limited to these two,

while seeking to buy time..." He opposed withdrawal or "bargain[ing] away Vietnam's security at the conference table."

Sorenson notes Kennedy's view that the stakes were high: "free world security," which would be severely compromised if Vietnam were lost and Southeast Asia were to fall to "the hungry Chinese." Kennedy's commitment to defend South Vietnam, Sorenson says, "was not only carried out but...reinforced by a vast expansion of effort." Impressed with Douglas MacArthur's opposition to sending troops, Kennedy preferred "a major counterinsurgency effort," though he "never made a final negative decision on troops" and "ordered the departments to be prepared for the introduction of combat troops should they prove to be necessary." Meanwhile, he "steadily expanded the size of the military assistance mission (2000 at the end of 1961, 15,500 at the end of 1963)[2] by sending in combat support units, air combat and helicopter teams, still more military advisers and instructors, and 600 of the green-hatted Special Forces to train and lead the South Vietnamese in anti-guerrilla tactics."

Like Schlesinger, Sorenson highlights JFK's hopeful January 1963 prediction that "the spear point of aggression has been blunted in Vietnam." But "In mid-1963 the picture worsened rapidly" with the repression of the Buddhists, Nhu's reported moves towards "a secret deal with the North," and his failure to heed US admonitions to "get back to the war." Worse yet was Nhu's public statement that "there were too many US troops in Vietnam." Even after the overthrow of the Diem-Nhu regime, "no early end to the Vietnam war was in sight" and "the struggle could well be, [JFK] thought, this nation's severest test of endurance and patience":

> He was simply going to weather it out, a nasty, untidy mess to which there was no other acceptable solution. Talk of abandoning so unstable an ally and so costly a commitment "only makes it easy for the Communists," said the President. "I think we should stay."

So Sorenson's account ends. Here too, there is no hint of any
intent to withdraw short of victory. Again, we may choose among
the same three conclusions.

No one was closer to JFK than his brother, the Attorney-
General. Sorenson notes that as RFK fully acknowledged, his
own role "was one of complete support for the U.S. commitment," which he had expressed in 1962: "The solution lies in our
winning it. This is what the President intends to do...We will remain here [in Saigon] until we do." In a 1964 oral history, RFK
said that the Administration had never faced the possibilities of
either withdrawal or escalation. Asked what JFK would have
done if the South Vietnamese appeared doomed, he said: "We'd
face that when we came to it." "Robert's own understanding of
his brother's position," his biographer Arthur Schlesinger reports,
was that "we should win the war" because of the domino effect.
RFK said further that by late 1963, the President had become
"very unhappy" with his dovish adviser Averell Harriman, who
was expressing skepticism about the optimistic reports from
Saigon. JFK's annoyance was so great that Harriman "put on
about ten years during that period...because he was so discour-
aged." If indeed JFK intended to withdraw without victory, he
was fooling both Harriman and his brother, it appears. The problem with Diem, RFK added, was that we need "somebody that
can win the war," and he wasn't the man for it. Accordingly, it is
no surprise that RFK fully supported Johnson's continuation of
what he understood to be his brother's policies through the 1965
escalation. By mid-1965 he was advocating negotiations while
condemning withdrawal. Schlesinger traces his break with Johnson's escalation policy to July 1965, Sorenson to February 1966.
He never proposed withdrawal, or indicated that his brother had
such a plan. According to Schlesinger, RFK's position as of
December 1965 was stated privately in these words: "I don't believe in pulling out the troops. We've got to show China we mean

to stop them. If we can hold them for about 20 years, maybe they will change the way Russia has."[3]

The last of the early accounts of the Kennedy Administration was written by Roger Hilsman, a representative of the dovish faction of the Administration (along with Harriman and Forrestal, he notes), and a high-ranking official particularly well-placed to know about Vietnam policy. He wrote shortly before the Tet Offensive, when the US troop level had peaked and protest against the war had reached a substantial scale, and well after severe doubts about the war were raised at the highest levels, including McNamara. (The latest source Hilsman cites is August 15, 1967.) Because of his position and the timing, Hilsman's account is of particular interest.

Hilsman takes it for granted that the goal throughout was "to defeat the Communist guerrillas," and speculates that the overthrow of Diem had offered "a second chance" to achieve this objective. Had JFK lived, "he might well have introduced United States ground forces into South Vietnam—though I believe he would not have ordered them to take over the war effort from the Vietnamese but would have limited their mission to the task of occupying ports, airfields, and military bases to demonstrate to the North Vietnamese that *they* could not win the struggle by escalation either"—the enclave strategy advocated by Ball and Taylor in early 1965, then publicly by General Gavin and others. Hilsman feels that LBJ "sincerely even desperately wanted to make the existing policy work," without US combat forces, citing LBJ's statement of September 25, 1964 that "We don't want our American boys to do the fighting for Asian boys"; to emphasize its importance, Hilsman also gives this LBJ quote as one of several opening his Vietnam section.[4] As we have seen, his conclusion about LBJ is supported by the internal record.

On withdrawal plans, Hilsman adds nothing of substance to what was published in the press at the time. His only comment

is that the optimistic predictions on which withdrawal was conditioned would come "to haunt Secretary McNamara and the
whole history of American involvement in Vietnam." The "real
tragedy," Hilsman writes, "is that many of the ranking American
officers in Saigon and the Pentagon believed it. "He reports his
feeling at the time that unless the Diem regime responded to US
pressure to dedicate itself to victory, or was replaced by generals
who would, "in six months to a year the Viet Cong would control
the country—or we would have to take over the war with American ground forces, which President Kennedy was convinced
would be a tragic error. But the real hell of it was that, even if
something did happen [in Saigon], the situation might still come
to that choice." The question of how to respond to a collapse of
the Saigon regime was delayed, in the hope that it would not
arise. "We'd face that when we came to it," as RFK put it in 1964.[5]

Hilsman's reservations about Johnson's war in this late 1967
account are subdued. He reports the objections he shared with
Harriman and Forrestal to Rostow's "well-reasoned case for a
gradual escalation," including ultimate bombing of the North,
the "fundamental" objection being "that it probably would not
work" (recall Forrestal's shift toward Rostow's position by March-
May 1964). He writes that the March 1964 memo that he sent
LBJ "as a sort of political testament on my departure concentrated on warning against the bombing of North Vietnam," a
highly contentious issue by late 1967. This reference to the
memo is not accurate. Bombing of the North is raised in only 3
of the 19 paragraphs. The memo concentrates on counterinsurgency, and secondarily, on ensuring "political stability" in Saigon,
where talk of "neutralization" must be terminated and a Marine
battalion might be dispatched to prevent another coup. With regard to bombing of the North, Hilsman's memo raised only tactical objections, calling for such bombing as a "useful *supplement*"
to counterinsurgency while repeating his recommendation of a

year earlier that covert actions against the North be continued, "keeping the threat of eventual destruction alive in Hanoi's mind." He also suggested "selected attacks on their infiltration bases and training camps" after sufficient progress had been made in suppressing the southern insurgency.[6]

In short, four years after the assassination, this dovish Vietnam policy insider has only limited objections to Johnson's already highly unpopular war. He praises LBJ for his "sincere" and "desperate" efforts to implement JFK's policies, and gives no indication that JFK planned to withdraw without victory, or had even considered withdrawal beyond his (tepid) authorization of McNamara's recommendations, based on the precondition of victory. He considers the withdrawal issue insignificant, so much so that he adds essentially nothing to what had been prominently published before the assassination. In retrospect, he feels that JFK might have made different choices than his senior advisers, but offers nothing to support that belief. Again, we face the same three alternatives, and are left only with the third as a plausible contender: the President had no plan to withdraw short of victory.

The internal record of 1964 shows that Kennedy doves saw matters much as described in the 1964-1967 memoirs, and therefore continued to support Johnson's policies, some pressing for further escalation, others (Ball, Mansfield) praising Johnson for choosing the middle course between escalation and withdrawal. All of this material adds further confirmation to the record of public statements and internal deliberations.

This completes the review of crucial evidence: the pre-Tet memoirs conform closely to the other sources of evidence. The conclusions are unambiguous, surprisingly so on a matter of current history: President Kennedy was firmly committed to the policy of victory that he inherited and transmitted to his successor, and to the doctrinal framework that assigned enormous significance to that outcome; he had no plan or intention to withdraw without victory; he had apparently given little thought to the matter altogether, and it was regarded as of marginal interest by those closest to him. Furthermore, the basic facts were prominently published at the time, with more detail than is provided by the early memoirs.

2. The Record Revised

By 1966, it was becoming clear that things were not going well in Vietnam. Arthur Schlesinger expressed concern that the US effort to "suppress the resistance" by widening the war had dubious prospects, though "we may all be saluting the wisdom and statesmanship of the American government" if Johnson's escalation succeeds, even if it leaves "the tragic country gutted and devastated by bombs, burned by napalm, turned into a wasteland by chemical defoliation, a land of ruin and wreck," with its "political and institutional fabric" pulverized. "No thoughtful American can withhold sympathy as President Johnson ponders the gloomy choices which lie ahead"—sympathy for the President, that is, not the victims. Referring to Joseph Alsop's predictions of victory, Schlesinger writes that "we all pray that Mr. Alsop will be right," though he doubts it. The only qualms are tactical: what will be the cost to us?

In this 1966 book, Schlesinger describes himself as keeping faith with JFK—plausibly enough. He proposes a "middle course": the indigenous resistance should surrender to the US and its client regime, accepting a US-run political process, such as the "valiant try at self-government" which "excited such idealistic hopes in the United States"; he is referring to the 1966 elections, in which the entire opposition (Communists and neutralists) was excluded from the ballot. Withdrawal, he says, is out of the question: it "would have ominous reverberations throughout Asia" and be "humiliating." We must, rather, abide by our "moral obligations" to our clients, "a new class of nouveaux mandarins...pervaded by nepotism, corruption and cynicism," and lacking popular support.[7]

Again we have the same alternatives: (1) Schlesinger is still concealing JFK's intent to withdraw without victory; (2) JFK had successfully concealed it from him; (3) There was no such intent, in which case his later claims are false.

Twelve years later, Schlesinger wrote that on January 6, 1966, Robert McNamara had privately informed him and other "New Frontier friends" that the US would have to seek "withdrawal with honor" in Vietnam. A few months later, the friends "decided to do what little we could to stir public opinion." His own contribution, he says, was to write *The Bitter Heritage*—which prays for victory and opposes withdrawal as unthinkable.[8]

After the Tet Offensive in January 1968, major domestic power sectors concluded that the enterprise was becoming too costly to sustain and called for it to be ended. Apart from the impact on the global economy, unfavorable to the US, the mounting popular opposition to the war was of particular concern. One part of the *Pentagon Papers* record that has gained little attention reviews the concern in high places that further escalation might lead to protest even beyond the "massive" demonstration at the Pentagon in October 1967, perhaps also large-scale civil disobedience. In considering further troop deployments, the Joint Chiefs wanted to ensure that "sufficient forces would still be available for civil disorder control," and the Defense Department feared that escalation might lead to "increased defiance of the draft and growing unrest in the cities," running the risk of "provoking a domestic crisis of unprecedented proportions."[9]

President Johnson was, in effect, dismissed from office, and policy was set towards disengagement.

The effect of the policy shift on the ideological system was dramatic. Virtually everyone suddenly turned out to have been an "early opponent of the war"—in secret, since no record can be found. In Cambridge, the home of the Kennedy "action in-tellectuals," it became a standing joke. A more accurate picture is given by the attitudes of the Massachusetts branch of Americans for Democratic Action, at the "ultraliberal" extreme. In late 1967, its leadership would not even accept membership applications from people they expected would speak in favor of an antiwar resolution sponsored by a local chapter that had fallen out of control.[10] A few weeks later, after the Tet Offensive, everything changed. By late 1969 the liberal press began to move beyond tactical complaints to critical comment, though with no serious deviation from state doctrine.[11]

Without too much oversimplification, we can take the Tet Offensive of January 1968 to be the turning point for the cultural managers, who now faced several challenging tasks. One was to defuse the opposition, an interesting story, still untold. Another was to restore the basic doctrines of the faith: The war must now be understood as a noble effort gone astray, in part because of disruptive domestic elements who had impeded the earnest efforts of "early opponents of the war." At the outer limits, we may say that the war began with "blundering efforts to do good," though "by 1969" it had become "clear to most of the world—and most Americans—that the intervention had been a disastrous mistake"; the argument against the war "was that the United States had misunderstood the cultural and political forces at work in Indochina—that it was in a position where it could not impose a solution except at a price too costly to itself" (Anthony Lewis).

Recall that the population never absorbed the lessons taught by the extreme doves, continuing to believe that the war was "fundamentally wrong and immoral," not a "mistake."

It is misleading to cite only those who have scaled the peaks of independent critical thought. More in the mainstream is Peter Kann of the *Wall Street Journal*, who concedes that 30 years ago there might have been an issue about "defending an often imperfect ally; supporting distant Asian dominoes; sowing democratic seeds in soil that frequently seemed infertile; waging the war with too much fire power, or too little." But today, "it is hard to think of any issue or any place in the world where hindsight offers a clearer spotlight in which to distinguish right from wrong." When we compare "free, prosperous and stable" countries like Indonesia that have been celebrating "personal dignity" since 1965 with the horrors of Indochina after our retreat, it is obvious to "common sense" that the hawks were right and those who saw the Communists as "groovy little people in the jungle" were dead wrong. That opponents of the war were supporters of Communism need not be argued. It follows at once from the basic doctrine of the Gospel according to Kann and associates: since US perfection is axiomatic and the concept of "US aggression and mass murder" meaningless gibberish, it follows that opponents of US policy are supporters of the hated enemy. As for the rest, putting aside the exaltation of atrocity and oppression, one wonders whether in some dark corner of Russia there remains some commissar so vile and cowardly as to proclaim the nobility of the Soviet cause in Afghanistan, pointing to the people of Kabul terrorized by the rockets of the rebel armies. If so, he can apply for a position at any American journal or university.

Given the power of the US propaganda system, as well as shared values, loyalists elsewhere uncritically adopt its doctrinal verities. The Washington bureau chief of the London *Economist* writes that "The war was a tragedy, which did much damage inside and outside America. But that is not at all the same thing as saying that it was wrong, and is very far from substantiating the view that those who believed the war was necessary were mistaken." The war may even have done a bit of damage to some heathen Indochinese, but the inheritors of centuries of British culture and experience do not tarry over such childish concerns.

The editors of the *Toronto Globe & Mail* caution the US not to overreach in its idealistic efforts to construct a new world order of heavenly virtue: "to career around the globe on a white charger invites disaster. (Remember Vietnam?)"[12] The debate over "humanitarian intervention" in late 1992 may have reached even lower depths of moral cowardice, with its musings on the "lessons of Vietnam," which showed how difficult such enterprises can be, how costly to us.

Gorbachev's Russia could face up to its crimes in Afghanistan, evoking much self-righteous smirking here. But the intellectual class in the United States, and their associates elsewhere, must acknowledge nothing and concede nothing. These are among the perquisites and responsibilities of power.

The dominant cast of mind was exhibited in the attempt to portray the media, which had always loyally supported the crusade and continued to do so, as dangerously adversarial, even a threat to the survival of free institutions. This application of the lesson taught by Tacitus (see page 8) was spearheaded by a two-volume Freedom House study of the Tet Offensive purporting to show that in their anti-establishment frenzy, the media had falsely portrayed an American victory as a defeat for the forces of freedom, thus undermining morale at home; the same charge was levelled against the Soviet media by the military and Communist Party hierarchy under Brezhnev, with no less merit. The conclusions of this "scholarly study" have become established doctrine, though it was demonstrated at once to be a pathetic mélange of falsehoods and fabrication, which reduces finally to the claim that the media were too "pessimistic" in their advocacy of the noble cause (though less pessimistic than US intelligence, the Pentagon, and the President's top advisers, as the Freedom House scholars chose not to say).[13]

For the totalitarian mind, adherence to state propaganda does not suffice: one must display proper enthusiasm while marching in the parade.

Interestingly, the media welcomed the Freedom House attack on their integrity, far preferring it to the readily-established truth: that they generally did their work with professional competence, but rarely straying from doctrinal purity. The preferred self-image is not the competent though compliant professional, but rather the anti-establishment crusader, who may go too far in the courageous defiance of power and institutions. Self-image aside, the crucial doctrinal goal is thereby achieved: discussion is bounded by the hawks, who say that the noble cause could have succeeded with better tactics, more commitment, and proper control over the "anti-Americans" who undermined it; and the doves, who "all prayed that the hawks would be right" but now see that our "blundering efforts to do good" were misplaced, an "error" based on misunderstanding and naiveté.

The high-level shift of policy after Tet called for a revision of the earlier record. Since everyone was now an "early opponent of the war," the same must have been true of the grand leader. The enterprise had soured; the picture of John F. Kennedy must therefore be modified. The Kennedy Administration was unusual in the role played by people sensitive to imagery and doctrine, and in a position to shape them. The love affair of the intellectual community with Camelot is in part a reaction to this unaccustomed whiff of (real or imagined) power. The liberal intelligentsia naturally felt the "need to insulate JFK from the disastrous consequences of the American venture in Southeast Asia," Thomas Brown observes in his study of Camelot imagery. "Kennedy's role in the Vietnam war is unsurprisingly...the aspect [of his public image and record] that has been subjected to the greatest number of revisions by Kennedy's admirers...The important thing was that JFK be absolved of responsibility for the Vietnam debacle; when the need for exculpation is so urgent, no obstacles—including morality and the truth—should stand in the way."[14]

No less important is another factor that Brown brings up in discussing the split among JFK's war managers over escalation: "The 'doves' in this debate," he notes, "were *not* advocates of complete withdrawal from Vietnam but of greater reliance on counterinsurgency measures." Termination of the attack against South Vietnam was unacceptable—indeed, unthinkable, the concept of US aggression being barred from the intellectual culture. To guard the faith, it is important to ensure that debate over the US war be constrained within the dove-hawk spectrum: the imaginable policy options lie between US-supported terror (allegedly JFK) and expansion of JFK's aggression to a full-scale attack on all of Indochina (LBJ, most of the Kennedy advisers who stayed on). And all choices must be sanitized: they are defense against "the assault from the inside" in JFK's words—the "assault" by indigenous guerrillas against a foreign-imposed terrorist regime that could not survive political competition. If discourse is constrained within these bounds, the propaganda system will have done its duty.

Brown's comments on such obstacles as "morality and the truth" relate specifically to one of the early post-Tet efforts to revise the image: White House aide Kenneth O'Donnell's 1972 memoir. Two of O'Donnell's stories have assumed center stage in the post-Tet reconstruction.[15] The first is that Kennedy had informed Senator Mansfield that he agreed with him "on the need for a complete military withdrawal from Vietnam." But he explained "that if he announced a withdrawal of American military personnel from Vietnam before the 1964 election, there would be a wild conservative outcry against returning him to the Presidency for a second term." The second is that afterwards, JFK made a private comment to O'Donnell that he presents verbatim:

> In 1965, I'll become one of the most unpopular Presidents in history. I'll be damned everywhere as a Communist appeaser. But I don't care. If I tried to pull out completely now from Vietnam, we would have an-

other Joe McCarthy scare on our hands, but I can do it after I'm reelected. So we had better make damned sure that I *am* reelected.

In 1975, Mansfield told columnist Jack Anderson that
Kennedy "was going to order a gradual withdrawal" but "never
had the chance to put the plan into effect," though he had "defi-
nitely and unequivocally" made that decision; in 1978, Mansfield
said further that Kennedy had informed him that troop withdrawal would begin in January 1964.[16] Noting Mansfield's (partial) confirmation of O'Donnell's report, Brown points out that
"one need not reject this story out of hand...to doubt that it was
a firm statement of Kennedy's intentions in Vietnam. Like many
politicians, JFK was inclined to tell people what they wanted to
hear." Every serious historian discounts such reports for the same
reason: "Kennedy probably told [Mansfield] what he wanted to
hear," Thomas Paterson observes. The same holds for other recollections, authentic or not, by political figures and journalists.

Whatever else he may have been, Kennedy was a political
animal, and knew enough to tell the Senate Majority Leader and
other influential people what they wanted to hear. He was also
keenly sensitive to the opposition to his policies among powerful
Senators, who saw them as harmful to US interests. The internal
record reveals that Kennedy left decisions on Vietnam largely in
the hands of his advisers. His own interventions express his "increasing concern" over the "need to make [an] effective case with
Congress for continued prosecution of the war," and to ensure
that congressional condemnation of Diem's repression "not end
up with a resolution requiring that we reduce aid" (September
1963). As for the media, "The way to confound the press is to
win the war."[17]

Kennedy was also aware that public support for the war was
thin, as were McNamara, Hilsman, and others. A year later, LBJ
won the election largely because of his outspoken opposition to
expanding the war. But JFK never saw the general discontent

among the public, press, and Congress as an opportunity to construct a popular base for withdrawal; rather, he sought to counter
it with extremist rhetoric about the grand stakes. Like McNamara, he hoped to bring the war to a successful end before discontent interfered with this plan. Had he intended to withdraw,
he would also have leaped at the opportunity provided by the
GVN call for reduction of forces (even outright withdrawal), and
its moves toward political settlement. As for the right-wing, a
President intent on withdrawal would have called upon highly-
respected military figures for support, including the most revered
figures of the far right.

The post-Tet O'Donnell-Mansfield version is that JFK intended to begin withdrawal in January 1964, but to complete it
only after his election, so as to fend off "another Joe McCarthy
scare." Even apart from the total lack of supporting evidence (and
the ample counterevidence), this story is hardly credible. Nothing
would have been better calculated to fan right-wing hysteria than
inflammatory rhetoric about the cosmic issues at stake, public
commitment to stay the course combined with withdrawal from
that commitment as the client regime collapsed in 1964, election
on the solemn promise to stand firm come what may, and then
completion of the withdrawal and betrayal. That plan would have
been sheer stupidity. Had Kennedy intended to withdraw, he
would have at least considered, and probably pursued, the course
just outlined. But there is no hint in the record that he gave that
possibility a moment's thought. Rather, he chose to enflame jingoist passions. The conclusions, again, seem rather clear.

The post-Tet recollections many years after the alleged conversations are subject to further question. Mansfield had not
called for "complete military withdrawal," so it is not possible for
JFK to have agreed with him on this. His actual advice was highly
qualified: the US should undertake a very limited withdrawal as
a "symbolic gesture" to warn Diem to get to business and win

the war. And he explicitly opposed withdrawal as LBJ took over. Furthermore, JFK rejected Mansfield's major recorded advice: to desist from public rhetoric about the great stakes in Indochina. The post-Tet recollections are not consistent with the internal record.

Far more credible, if one chooses to take such material seriously, is General Wheeler's recollection in 1964 (not years later, in a period of ideological reconstruction) that Kennedy was interested in extending the war to North Vietnam.

Furthermore, O'Donnell's and Mansfield's belated accounts are virtually meaningless, even if taken at face value. JFK's qualified endorsement of the McNamara-Taylor recommendations on withdrawal was made public at once. Perhaps, years later, Mansfield and O'Donnell had forgotten the withdrawal plans that were prominently published; recall that these seemed so insignificant to JFK's close associates and chroniclers that they scarcely mention them, if at all. The only novelty in these private communications would have been if JFK had stated that he knew that the optimistic assessments were false, and was going to withdraw anyway, which is, indeed, the way these alleged communications are interpreted by Newman, Schlesinger, and other post-Tet advocates of the withdrawal-without-victory thesis. On a thread that thin, one can hang nothing.

Despite such obvious flaws, the O'Donnell-Mansfield stories are taken very seriously by Kennedy hagiographers.

The Camelot memoirists proceeded to revise their earlier versions after Tet, separating JFK (and by implication, themselves) from what had happened. Sorenson was the first. In the earlier version, Kennedy was preparing for the introduction of combat troops if necessary and intended to "weather it out" come what may, not abandoning his ally, who would have collapsed without large-scale US intervention. Withdrawal is not discussed. Diplomacy is considered a threat, successfully overcome by the overthrow of the

Diem government. But post-Tet, Sorenson is "convinced" that JFK would have sought diplomatic alternatives in 1965—with the client regime in still worse straits, as he notes. Furthermore, for unexamined reasons, JFK would have made a more realistic cost-benefit analysis than did his trusted associates, who continued to run the war for LBJ as they had for him. "I believe he would have devoted increasing time...in the winter of 1963-1964 and found an answer" to the question of how to get out of Vietnam, Sorenson says, not telling us what this answer might have been as the US-GVN position rapidly deteriorated, and not recalling his own advice to LBJ while he was still on the White House staff: to avoid any hint of wavering in the pursuit of victory because of the enormous stakes (January 1964).

The October 1963 withdrawal plan, unmentioned in the old version, assumes great significance in Sorenson's post-Tet revision. Kennedy "did authorize, as an indication of his goal, the October 1963 statement by McNamara and Taylor predicting a withdrawal of most American military advisors by the end of 1965, beginning late in 1963," Sorenson writes, failing to add that in 1965 he [Sorenson] had found these steps unworthy of mention, that Kennedy refused to commit himself to the plan, that withdrawal was explicitly contingent on military success, and that the plan called for intensification of the war and stood alongside the effort to replace Diem if he would not "focus on winning the war" as JFK demanded. Sorenson also says that Kennedy "made it very clear that any suggestion from the Saigon government that our forces were unwelcome would start them 'on their way home...the day after it was suggested'." That JFK made such statements is true; that he and his associates regarded such suggestions with dismay and sought to block them in every way is also true, as we have seen.[18]

Arthur Schlesinger entered the lists in 1978 with his biography of Robert Kennedy. Unlike Sorenson, he does not confine himself to speculation about JFK's intent. Rather, he constructs a new history, radically revising his own earlier version.[19]

In the pre-Tet history, General MacArthur's views merit a passing phrase as an "opinion" offered the President. There is no indication that JFK paid the slightest attention; they are not mentioned in the 600 pages that follow. In the post-Tet version, we read:

> In late April, Kennedy discovered an unexpected ally—General Douglas MacArthur, who assured him that it would indeed be a "mistake" to fight in Southeast Asia. "He thinks," the President dictated in a rare *aide-mémoire*," our line should be Japan, Formosa and the Philippines... He said that the 'chickens are coming home to roost' from Eisenhower's years and I live in the chicken coop."

By April 1992, we discover that *A Thousand Days* had recorded JFK's "delight in General MacArthur's opposition to a land war in Asia," a surprise to the reader of the earlier version.[20]

Pre-Tet, it was JFK and Arthur Schlesinger who rejoiced over the defeat of "aggression" in Vietnam in 1962. Post-Tet, it is the *New York Times* that absurdly denounces "Communist 'aggression' in Vietnam," while "Kennedy was determined to stall." And though RFK did call for victory over the aggressors in 1962, he was deluded: he was following "the party line as imparted to him by McNamara and Taylor," failing to understand the huge gap between the President's views and the McNamara-Taylor party line—which Schlesinger had attributed to the President, with his own endorsement, in the pre-Tet version. The post-Tet revision offers no explanation for these innovations, or for JFK's decision to delegate responsibility to run the war to one of the men who peddled the party line he so disdained, while promoting the other to Chairman of the Joint Chiefs—a curious reaction to their betrayal of the President's cause.

The doves are identified as Harriman, Hilsman, and Forrestal, who called for counterinsurgency and social reform, not escalation. Nothing is said about their doctrine that "there are no quitters here" or their actual role in the Kennedy Administration, reviewed earlier; or their later thoughts as optimistic assessments changed. True, all the details were not in the public domain in 1978, though enough was; and it is hard to believe that an Administration insider would not have had at least the general picture.[21]

In the post-Tet version, the Joint Chiefs join the *New York Times*, McNamara, and Taylor as extremists undermining the President's moderate policies. Commenting on JCS Chairman General Lyman Lemnitzer's invocation of the "well-known commitment to take a forthright stand against Communism in Southeast Asia," Schlesinger writes sardonically that "For the Chiefs the commitment may have been 'well-known.' But they had thus far failed in their efforts to force it on the President"—who regularly voiced it in still more strident terms. Many examples have been cited, including Schlesinger's own report of the President's fears of upsetting "the whole world balance" if the US were to retreat in Vietnam. Or, we may recall JFK's summer 1963 comment on the need to establish a "stable government" in South Vietnam and to support its "struggle to maintain its national independence": "for us to withdraw from that effort would mean a collapse not only of South Vietnam but Southeast Asia. So we are going to stay there." These were "temperate words" in Schlesinger's pre-Tet version. Compare Lemnitzer.[22]

In his laudatory 1992 review of Newman's book, Schlesinger joins Newman in casting blame on military crazies. Both cite what Schlesinger calls "a hysterical [January] 1962 memorandum" (and Newman describes as "extraordinary") in which the Joint Chiefs predict "that 'the fall of South Vietnam to Communist control would mean the eventual Communist domination of all of the Southeast Asian mainland' and that most of Asia would capitulate to what the military still stubbornly called the 'Sino-Soviet Bloc'."

"Such hyperbole confirmed Kennedy's low opinion of the military," Schlesinger writes. Checking back to the pre-Tet version, we read that it was JFK's *State Department* that babbled on about the "Sino-Soviet Bloc" while Kennedy in 1963 regarded China as the "long-term danger to the peace"; the USSR, in contrast, was merely the "monolithic and ruthless conspiracy" intent on world conquest. The Chiefs' "hyperbole" about South Vietnam, furthermore, sounds pretty tame in comparison to JFK's own rhetoric, as we have seen.[23]

To illustrate Kennedy's moderation and concern for social reform in contrast to the military, Schlesinger cites the 1956 speech quoted earlier (page 57), excising its inflammatory content, which George Ball described as "one of [JFK's] more purple passages" with "a whole bagful of well-worn metaphors" about dominos and huge stakes.[24]

In Schlesinger's pre-Tet book on John F. Kennedy (1965, 1967), there was only a bare mention of withdrawal plans, with no indication that JFK had ever considered the matter (recall that the basic facts were public knowledge). There is no hint that anyone considered withdrawal without victory. In his 1966 "anti-war" book *The Bitter Heritage*, still pre-Tet, Schlesinger rejects withdrawal outright, upholding JFK's banner, he claims.

The post-Tet biography of Robert Kennedy (1978) is radically different. Here JFK's alleged withdrawal plans merit a full chapter, even though the book is not devoted to JFK but to his brother, whose "involvement in Vietnam had been strictly limited before Dallas" and "was nonexistent" after, Schlesinger tells us. This startling difference between the pre- and post-Tet versions is not attributed to any significant new information, indeed is not mentioned at all. Schlesinger's explanation for the chapter on withdrawal is that "because [RFK] later had to struggle with his brother's Vietnam legacy, it is essential to understand what that legacy was." Perhaps. But one would then want to know why the legacy appears nowhere in the pre-Tet publications.

In 1992, Schlesinger went a step further, claiming that he had put forth the JFK withdrawal thesis all along.[25]

Post-Tet, the October 1963 decisions, emerging from their earlier obscurity, become "the first application of Kennedy's phased withdrawal plan," as Kennedy masterfully withstands efforts by his aides to deepen the US commitment, to limit his flexibility, and to delete any reference to troop withdrawal (Schlesinger's sources are oral reports, with little relation to the documentary record, imaginative readings apart; the New York Times account of 1963 was more informative). JFK's plan to withdraw, unmentioned before, now serves as prime evidence that he had separated himself from the two main "schools": the advocates of counterinsurgency and the purveyors of the McNamara-Taylor "party line." He was opposed to "both win-the-war factions,...vaguely searching for a nonmilitary solution." His undeviating public call for winning the war is apparently to be understood as a ploy to deflect the right-wing; his equally insistent call for victory in the internal record is unmentioned.

Overriding the objection of the Chiefs, Schlesinger writes, in July 1962 "Kennedy instructed McNamara to start planning for the phased withdrawal of American military personnel"; in the pre-Tet version, we read only about the optimism of Harkins and McNamara in mid-1962, with no mention of any withdrawal plan (896). Post-Tet, the July 1962 instructions were the origin of the October 1963 plan, which, for the President, put a limit on escalation and was "the reserve plan for extrication," though the disruptive generals saw it only "as a means of putting pressure on Diem"—as did Mansfield and other doves, and Schlesinger in his marginal pre-Tet reference to McNamara's recommendation.

As we have already seen, the July 1962 instructions were predicated on the assumption that victory was within reach and that any delay beyond 1965 would make it difficult to contain domestic opposition to the war. In short, JFK's goal was withdrawal *after victory*—by mid-1965, McNamara thought, though to the end, JFK remained unwilling to commit himself. The top military command disagreed only in that they were more optimistic, expecting to wind it up in a year. All this is omitted, though the basic facts were available in the *Pentagon Papers*.

Continuing with the post-Tet version, Schlesinger writes that by 1963, withdrawal was turning from a "precaution...into a preference." That is what "the evidence suggests." What the evidence actually suggests is that withdrawal was *always* a preference, but only after victory; and so it remained in 1963. The evidence that Schlesinger cites is the O'Donnell-Mansfield material, already discussed. His only further evidence is Kennedy's public statement in September 1963 that "it is their war. They are the ones who have to win it or lose it...." Recall that this point was made to the President by his top military commander in Vietnam, General McGarr, in February 1962, and was reiterated after the assassination by LBJ, McNamara, and Generals Westmoreland and Taylor. By the same logic, they must have shared JFK's secret intent.

By late summer of 1963, the post-Tet version continues, "Kennedy was still playing out his public hand while secretly wondering how to get out"—so secretly that no trace is left in the record and his closest associates knew nothing about it; the "public hand" was the inflammatory rhetoric that could only serve to undermine withdrawal. On November 14, Schlesinger reports, Kennedy told a press conference "somewhat confusedly" that the upcoming Honolulu conference would focus on "how we can intensify the struggle, how we can bring Americans out of there. Now that is our object, to bring Americans home." The confusion results from "Kennedy's private determination to begin, at whatever cost, a strategy of extrication," a doctrine for which not a particle of evidence has been adduced. With that doctrine abandoned, JFK's statement unconfusedly reflects his awareness of domestic discontent and his commitment to intensify the war and withdraw after victory, explicit in the internal and public record.

Schlesinger notes that "In May 1963 Nhu proposed publicly that the United States start withdrawing its troops," adding that "sooner or later we Vietnamese will settle our differences between us." He reports inaccurately that Nhu's hints about treating with Hanoi were not "taken seriously in either Saigon or Washington" (citing William Bundy); the record shows that they were taken quite seriously, and were a factor in the Kennedy Administration decision to overthrow the government. "No one knew then whether the explorations had any reality," Schlesinger adds correctly, without, however, giving the reason: JFK and his advisers feared that these explorations had all too much reality, and acted to destroy the threat, another crucial fact that undermines the withdrawal-without-victory thesis. A "Diem-Ho deal could have been the means of an American exit from Vietnam in 1963," Schlesinger correctly observes, so that "An opportunity of some sort was perhaps missed"—though not because of ignorance, as he suggests. Rather, it was understood that such a deal would force the US to withdraw without victory.

Post-Tet, Schlesinger adopts the thesis that the assassination of the President led to a dramatic reversal of policy.[26] He argues that LBJ abandoned JFK's withdrawal plans at once, shifting to escalation. His evidence is the opening paragraph of NSAM 273 of November 26:

> It *remains* the *central objective* of the United States in South Vietnam to assist the people and Government of that country to *win* their contest against the *externally directed* and supported communist conspiracy.

Schlesinger highlights these words to show that LBJ was undertaking "both the total commitment Kennedy had always refused and the diagnosis of the conflict" that Kennedy had "never quite accepted." The highlighted words appear regularly in both the public and private Kennedy record, as does the diagnosis; numerous examples have already been given, including JFK's own demand that everyone must "focus on winning the war." The draft of NSAM 273 written before the assassination by Kennedy's top advisers, expressing his policies, opens with the same paragraph.[27] The October 2 White House statement approving the McNamara-Taylor recommendations is hardly different. The hidden meanings and implications are in the eye of the beholder.

Schlesinger also claims that by emphasizing that American military programs "should be maintained at levels as high as those in the time of the Diem regime," NSAM 273 "nullified Kennedy's extrication intent." His source is the *Pentagon Papers* analysis (III, 18), which makes clear that it is the aid programs that are being discussed and that the statement "served to indicate continuance by the new President of policies already agreed upon." Schlesinger's source continues: "The objectives of the United States with respect to the withdrawal of U.S. military personnel remain as stated in the White House statement of October 2, 1963." As noted, that White House public statement had also emphasized that "Major U.S. assistance" would be maintained as long as needed by the client regime. The phrase Schlesinger cites from NSAM 273 nullifies no "extrication intent," in fact changes nothing.

Schlesinger's account of what followed is hardly more persuasive. Thus he cites a high-level Kennedy official as writing that the Kennedy brothers *"regarded Vietnam as a massive source of vexation and concern but not as intrinsically important in itself—only as a counter in a larger game."* These words, which Schlesinger again highlights, are supposed to prove that "As civilized, well-educated Americans they were totally devoid of the obsessive attitudes that characterized President Johnson under the influence of the 'hardliners'"; the wording expresses the boundless contempt of the

Kennedy intellectuals for the boorish Texas interloper defacing the elegance of Camelot. The cited phrase is from 1970, post-Tet; a page earlier, Schlesinger had quoted a letter from RFK to Johnson in June 1964 in which he described Vietnam as "obviously the most important problem facing the United States."[28] As for the "obsessive attitudes" expressed by JFK and his top advisers, enough has already been said. Finally, it was Kennedy's personally-chosen and trusted senior advisers who were influencing LBJ and directing his war, with his brother's firm support, until things began to go awry.

Schlesinger elaborates in his 1992 review of Newman's book. Endorsing Newman's "withdrawal without victory" thesis, Schlesinger writes that he himself had made the same point in his *A Thousand Days*, where he reported JFK's view that "it was a Vietnamese war. If we converted it into a white man's war, we would lose." He does not mention that LBJ later made similar remarks: we do not want "our American boys to do the fighting for Asian boys," he proclaimed during the 1964 election campaign—not quite the same as the JFK-Schlesinger version because for LBJ, it was a point of principle, while for JFK-Schlesinger, it was sheer expedience, a question of how to win. Furthermore, as noted, the same point had been made by the military command before and after. The sharp pre- vs. post-Tet contrast again passes unexamined.

The third pre-Tet Kennedy memoirist, Roger Hilsman, has written several letters to the press responding to critics of the withdrawal thesis, in the course of its 1991-1992 revival. In them, he takes a stronger stand on JFK's intent to withdraw than in his pre-Tet discussion.[29] But a close reading shows that Hilsman is careful to evade the crucial questions. He says that JFK wanted to withdraw, which is undeniable; so did Rostow and LeMay—after victory. He says also that JFK was determined not to let it become an American war. The same is true generally of his advisers, who then did just that as circumstances drastically changed, leaving them no other choice, they concluded, on the premises they shared with JFK. While serving in the LBJ Administration, Hilsman largely agreed, as we have seen. Hilsman's current interventions skirt the issues, only clouding them further.

Consider Hilsman's latest intervention in the debate, as I write.[30] Here he addresses the charge that he waited until 1992 to make it public "that President Kennedy intended to withdraw from Vietnam." Not true, Hilsman responds. Kennedy himself had made this clear in his news conference of September 2, 1963, in which he said that "In the final analysis it is their war. They have to win it or lose it." After the assassination, he continues, Johnson "made it clear to people in his administration dealing with Vietnam that he had dropped Kennedy's last three words": that is, he would not allow the war to be lost. Hilsman then refers to his objections to LBJ's decision to bomb North Vietnam, offered "most extensively" in his 1967 book. He claims further that "it is difficult to make yourself heard," alleging suppression by media and historians of Hilsman's efforts to inform them "that Kennedy, before his death, had begun to implement a plan to withdraw from Vietnam." Defense rests.

Note that Hilsman adduces no evidence that Kennedy intended to withdraw from Vietnam without victory, the only point at issue. The charge of suppression is not particularly convincing; surely Hilsman could have found some journal willing to allow him a few words. That aside, he had nothing to make public: the initiation of the withdrawal plan had been prominently reported in October 1963, less fully in his 1967 book. Furthermore, his objections to LBJ's bombing in that book are hardly "extensive." Indeed they are quite pallid, as we have seen; hardly a surprise, since he himself had called for measured escalation against the North while serving in the JFK and LBJ Administrations. Finally, consider the claim that LBJ dropped the last three words in JFK's statement that "They have to win it or lose it." To claim on the basis of these three words that Kennedy intended to withdraw without victory makes as much sense as to attribute the same intention to LBJ on the basis of his statement, a year later, opposing the dispatch of US troops. Or to attribute the same intention to the top US military command throughout, on the basis of similar statements. That is why Hilsman makes no such claim in his 1967 memoir, in which he emphasizes LBJ's statement that "We don't want our American boys to do the fighting for Asian boys" to show his "sincere" and "desperate" effort to carry out JFK's plans. Recall also Hilsman's observation in his 1967 book that 10 days after the three-word deletion on which he now hangs his case, JFK's public commitment to "win the war" and not "see a war lost" became "a policy guideline," as, indeed, he had recognized a few days after in internal planning (see pages 58 and 94).

However informative they may be with regard to the tasks of cultural management, the post-Tet revisions by leading Kennedy intellectuals have no value as history. Rather, they *constitute* a chapter of cultural history, one that is of no slight interest, I believe.

The post-Tet reconstruction is highly serviceable, therefore likely to endure irrespective of fact, at least in circles that derive their inspiration and imagery from Camelot. By early 1993, it was gaining the status of background information. Thus in reviewing a biography of Robert McNamara in the *Boston Globe*, Robert Kuttner writes that though McNamara had been "taken in by the bogus statistics supplied by Gen. Paul Harkins," by late 1963 his "powers of skepticism revived." "With Kennedy, he embraced a plan to increase assistance but turn the show over to the Vietnamese, win or lose, by 1965."

In the biography under review, Deborah Shapley is much more cautious. McNamara told her that he and Kennedy had agreed to withdraw without victory, Shapley writes, but she found herself suspecting that "his sincere belief that Kennedy would have gotten out of Vietnam was something he arrived at later when the war had become tragic and traumatic for him and the nation." His "reverence for John Kennedy" might have led him "to self-deceive, to believe that his hero and mentor would have wisely guided them out." "No hard evidence for McNamara's claim has come to light." "Hard evidence" is substantial, but as we have seen, it consistently undermines the claim. Shapley writes that McNamara and Kennedy "may have had a different, private agenda"; her sources are Newman and Schlesinger's "interesting theory" of 1978, concocted without a shred of evidence or a word about the still more interesting pre-Tet silence. All other sources cited are post-Tet, in part second-hand: private reminiscences of 1970 (Gilpatric) and 1986 (McNamara), and current interviews.[31]

In short, the belief remains pure faith, held in the face of abundant counter-evidence from every relevant source.

3. The Hero-Villain Scenario

The withdrawal-without-victory thesis is typically understood to subsume a second one: that LBJ immediately reversed policy from withdrawal to escalation; NSAM 263 (October 11) and NSAM 273 (November 26, with a pre-assassination draft) are commonly adduced in evidence, but they sustain no such conclusion. The major effort to establish the dual thesis is John Newman's book. As noted, this "ten year study" received much attention and praise, over a broad spectrum. It was the basis for the influential Oliver Stone film *JFK*, and is taken by much of the left to be a definitive demonstration of the twin theses. The book was strongly endorsed by Arthur Schlesinger, who describes it as a "solid contribution," with its "straightforward and workmanlike, rather military...organization, tone and style" and "meticulous and exhaustive examination of documents." Former CIA Director William Colby, who headed the Far East division of the CIA in

1963-1964, hailed Newman's study of these years as a "brilliant, meticulously researched and fascinating account of the decision-making which led to America's long agony in Vietnam"; *America's agony*, in accordance with approved doctrine.[32]

The book is not without interest. It contains some new documentary evidence, which further undermines the Newman-Schlesinger thesis when extricated from the chaotic jumble of materials interlarded with highlighted phrases that demonstrate nothing, confident interpretations of private intentions and beliefs, tales of intrigue and deception of extraordinary scale and complexity, so well-concealed as to leave no trace in the record, and conclusions that become more strident as the case collapses before the author's eyes. By the end, he claims that the National Security Council meetings of 1961 "more than resolve the question" of whether Kennedy would have sent combat troops under the radically different circumstances faced by his advisers in 1965, a conclusion that captures accurately the level of argument.

Newman's basic contention seems to be that JFK was surrounded by evil advisers who were trying to thwart his secret plan to withdraw without victory, though unaccountably, he kept giving them more authority and promoting them to higher positions, perhaps because he didn't understand them. Thus JFK thought that Taylor was "the one general...who shared his own views and that he could, therefore, trust to carry out his bidding." Shamelessly deceived, JFK therefore placed him in charge of the Special Group on counterinsurgency, promoted him to Chairman of the Joint Chiefs, and relied on him until the end, though Taylor was undermining him at every turn; Taylor became "the second most powerful person in the White House," Newman observes, making no attempt to resolve the paradox. From the beginning, the "record leaves the reader with the unforgettable image of a President pitted against his own advisors and the bureaucracy that served under him."[33]

There are a few "good guys," but in the chaos, it is hard to be sure who they are: perhaps Harriman, Forrestal, Hilsman, and McNamara, though even they joined the malefactors who beset our hero on every side (Harriman and Hilsman "mired Kennedy in a plot to overthrow Diem" [346], etc.). McNamara's role in these imaginative constructions is particularly intriguing. On November 26, 1961, Newman explains, Kennedy took command of officialdom in the "Thanksgiving Day Massacre," carrying out "a sweeping change of personnel" so that his own men would be in a position to implement his plans. "The person who emerged that day as Kennedy's point man on the Vietnam War was Robert Strange McNamara"—who, at a meeting three weeks earlier, had taken a prominent role in favor of deploying US military forces in Vietnam, and was "still anticipating a decision to commit U.S. combat forces," as he advocated, on November 13. On November 26, McNamara was therefore made "personally responsible" for executing the President's policies. And so he did, we read: McNamara "was determined to execute the Commander-in-Chief's intent: a genuine withdrawal from Vietnam" (October 1963). As in the case of Taylor's rise to the top, no explanation is given for these curious shifts and decisions, or for McNamara's role under LBJ.[34]

The withdrawal-without-victory thesis rests on the assumption that Kennedy realized that the optimistic military reports were incorrect—or, as Newman claims, an elaborate effort to deceive the President. Newman's treatment of this issue is therefore central to the story.

Closely paraphrasing the account in the *Pentagon Papers*, reviewed above, he describes the July 1962 events as the beginning of "the lengthy paper trail on the Kennedy withdrawal plan for Vietnam." By then, he writes, "The Americans were ready to declare victory and come home," and expected to bring "the Vietnam problem 'to a successful conclusion within a reasonable time'." McNamara gave Harkins instructions to "come up with a plan to wrap things up and come home" (Newman). Harkins considered the war almost over, but McNamara urged that "we must assume the worst," taking the "conservative view" that "it will take three years instead of one year" and making plans accordingly. Unequivocally, the goal was withdrawal *after victory*, by 1965.

Into the fall of 1962, Newman writes, "the deception was working, and Kennedy, like McNamara, had come to believe the perception delivered by the uninterrupted string of false reports emanating from Vietnam." But by March 1963, JFK had "figured out...that the success story was a deception." There is "hard evidence" for this, he claims, citing an NBC documentary eight months later that questioned the optimistic intelligence reports. The remainder of the evidence is that "in his heart he must have known" that the military program was a failure. Unlike his advisers (at least, those not in on the various "deceptions"), Kennedy "had to notice when the military myth was shaken by Bowles and Mendenhall in late 1962," and by Mansfield's pessimism. "When the drama of the Wheeler versus Hilsman-Forrestal match ended up in his office in February 1963, the implication that the story of success was untrue could no longer be overlooked" (by JFK, uniquely); the "drama" is the difference of judgment as to the time scale for victory, already reviewed (see pages 86-89).

These conclusions are presented on faith. A closer look shaves the sliver of evidence even further. Consider the timing. We read that "By the fall of 1962 the deception was working," but JFK "had to notice" the reports of Bowles and Mendenhall "in late 1962"—in fact, in *August* 1962. Putting that problem aside, both of these reports are ambiguous, and Mendenhall's, as Newman notes, "did not go higher than the Deputy Assistant Secretary of State for Far Eastern Affairs"; it is unclear, then, how JFK "had to notice" it. As for Bowles, he had been cut out of policymaking sectors long before. Unmentioned is the further fact that Bowles visited Vietnam in July 1963 and sent a highly confidential report to McGeorge Bundy, which, in this case, the President may have seen. Bowles wrote that "the military situation is steadily improving" although "the political situation is rapidly deteriorating," repeating the standard view. He also warned that "We cannot achieve our objectives in Southeast Asia as long as Diem and his family run Vietnam." He recommended that the US support someone who will "overthrow Diem" and send "U.S. special service troops and advisors into Laos to beef up and train the best Laotian troops," using Thai mercenaries and ARVN as well for this purpose; he also appears to be calling for Thailand to occupy part of northwestern Laos, though some sentences are not declassified. With "a bit of luck," we may "turn the tide" and "lay the basis for a far more favorable situation in Southeast Asia than seemed possible a few months ago."[35]

On these grounds, we are to conclude that JFK alone understood that official optimism was unwarranted.

Curiously, there actually is one bit of evidence that supports the desired conclusion, but Newman and other advocates of the thesis do not make use of it. Recall that at the NSC meeting considering the McNamara-Taylor recommendations, Kennedy dissociated himself from the plan to withdraw 1,000 personnel because he did not want to be "accused of being over optimistic" in case the military situation did not make withdrawal feasible. He allowed the sentence on withdrawal to remain only if attributed to McNamara and Taylor, without his acquiescence. In public too he was more hesitant about the withdrawal plan than the military command, as we have seen. One might argue, then, that JFK did not share the optimism of his advisers, and was therefore unwilling to commit himself to withdrawal. This conclusion has two merits not shared by the thesis we are examining: (1) it has some evidence to support it; (2) it conforms to the general picture of Kennedy's commitment to military victory provided by the internal record.

Newman takes a different course, however, asserting that
JFK "had disassociated himself from the optimistic McNamara-
Taylor timetable because he could not yet know whether his withdrawal would be conducted under a winning or a losing
battlefield situation." Whatever this is supposed to mean, Newman ignores the reason Kennedy actually gave: that "if we were
not able to take this action by the end of this year, we would be
accused of being over optimistic." This treatment of the evidence
illustrates Newman's technique precisely. Given the dogma that
JFK planned to withdraw without victory, all evidence to the contrary proves that he was being "brilliant...and duplicitous," cleverly concealing from his top advisers the truth about what was
"in his heart." Adopting the same procedure, Newman concludes
that "Kennedy decided, apparently...in February or March 1963,
to get out of Vietnam even if it meant the war would be lost."
Evidence is nil, and counterevidence substantial, but irrelevant,
thanks to the analytic technique.

To establish his thesis, Newman ignores the internal record
of JFK's interventions and relies heavily (in the end, almost exclusively) on O'Donnell's 1972 report and Mansfield's later comments (1975, 1978). O'Donnell's story, Newman writes, "makes
it abundantly clear that Kennedy knew the war was a lost cause,
and that his problem was how to disguise his intentions until
after the election." Newman declares further that "there is no
doubt that Kennedy made these confidential remarks" reported
by Mansfield and O'Donnell. These remarks must therefore be
placed "side by side" with JFK's public comments, which, Newman agrees, flatly contradict them. When we compare the public
comments and the "confidential remarks" to O'Donnell and
Mansfield, Newman writes, "the purpose for his remarks at these
press conferences become [sic] clear: they were calculated to
throw off his political opponents and the supporters of massive
U.S. intervention."[36]

Contrary to this remarkable reasoning, there is ample reason to be skeptical about these post-Tet reconstructions years after the alleged conversations. They are furthermore implausible and largely meaningless, hence discounted by historians generally. They do not begin to compare in significance with the extensive internal record and the public statements of the President, which conform to the internal record, a crucial fact missing from this study. In fact, they are far less significant than the pre-Tet memoirs and oral history, which Newman also ignores. As for the "calculation" on which the Newman-Schlesinger thesis rests, that makes no sense at all, as already discussed.

No more impressive is Newman's faith in a "riveting talk with President Kennedy" described by Senator Wayne Morse ten years later (reported verbatim in the press, and by Newman), in which JFK allegedly told the Senate's leading opponent of the war that he agreed with him. Whatever the plausibility of the story, it is devoid of significance, for reasons understood by every historian: a President may well tell an influential Senator in private what he would like to hear, while heeding other voices.[37]

Newman's tale is woven from dark hints and "intrigue," with "webs of deception" at every level. Subtitles read: "A DECEPTION WITHIN THE DECEPTION," "THE DEEPENING WEB OF DECEPTION," "THE DECEIVERS AND THE DECEIVED," etc. The military were deceiving Kennedy's associates who were deceiving Kennedy, while he in turn was deceiving the public and his advisers, and many were deceiving themselves. At least, I think that is what the story is supposed to be; it is not easy to tell in this labyrinth of fancy.

LBJ is portrayed as one of the really bad guys, in conformity with the thesis of a sharp policy change after the assassination (or worse, according to the darker version). The evidence? On intervention in Laos, "ONLY LBJ SUPPORTED [Admiral] BURKE," a section heading reads, supported only by Burke's recollection in oral history 6 years later that LBJ said "he thought I had something, but that was because he spoke first, perhaps."[38]

Later comes an "intrigue" too intricate to unravel that is supposed to show how LBJ put one over on the unsuspecting JFK, advancing the nefarious plan to introduce combat troops. The plot only thickens when we find that LBJ's recommendation was: "do not get bogged down, Mr. President, in a land war in Southeast Asia" (Johnson's military aide Colonel Burris). There is an "inconsistency," Newman concedes, offering an explanation supported only by the need to establish LBJ's devious role. Complicating the matter further, "Johnson chose to distance himself from the combat troops idea while simultaneously advocating a commitment that might well require they be sent in the future" (exactly like his boss), perhaps exploiting Kennedy's "impulsive innocence." LBJ's written report to the President "finessed the ticklish problem of U.S. combat troops by saying this might have to be faced at 'some point'," Newman writes. LBJ wrote that "Asian leaders do not want them 'at this time'...Combat troops were not required or desirable..." A subtle rascal, "Johnson then cleverly avoided a definitive statement on troops by framing the question as a choice between U.S. support or complete disengagement."

As a further complication, "Johnson didn't really want to get involved in Vietnam" in the first place (Colonel Burris).

In fact, Newman observes, LBJ played no role in Vietnam policy after May 1961. The reason, we are told with the usual confidence, is that he "went underground" because "He had his own aspirations for the White House, and getting out of the limelight was the most prudent thing to do." Maybe, maybe not. Before he went underground, he had been treated with utter contempt, simply ordered to go to Vietnam (where he allegedly carried out his evil plot) over his vociferous objections.[39]

LBJ enters the story again at a White House meeting of August 31, 1963, where he complains that he is not being informed and expresses doubts about the planned coup, "harsh and aggressive remarks" (actually, mild objections) that "had a chilling effect," as "attested to by the fact that no one said anything in reply"—presumably because the Kennedy intellectuals considered him a Texas lout.[40]

The picture of LBJ the sinister plotter is a fundamental part of Newman's theory about the "reversal of intent with respect to combat troops" as LBJ took the reins after the assassination. Here is Newman's crucial evidence:

> A comment that Lyndon Johnson made in December [1963] underlines the far-reaching and profound nature of this reversal and demonstrates how the tragedy of Dallas affected the course of the Vietnam War. While Kennedy had told O'Donnell in the spring of 1963 that he could not pull out of Vietnam until he was reelected, "So we had better make damned sure I *am* reelected," at a White House reception on Christmas eve, a month after he succeeded to the presidency, Lyndon Johnson told the Joint Chiefs: "Just let me get elected and then you can have your war."

Truly a dramatic demonstration of a historic reversal—until we check the source, Stanley Karnow's popular book *Vietnam*, which is "loosely sourced," Newman observes elsewhere, disparaging it when Karnow questioned the thesis of the Stone film. Putting aside doubts about reliability and about "what Kennedy had told O'Donnell," here is what Newman's source says about LBJ and the White House reception:

> [Johnson] knew that Pentagon lobbyists, among the best in the business, could persuade conservatives in Congress to sabotage his social legislation unless he satisfied their demands. As he girded himself for the 1964 presidential campaign, he was especially sensitive to the jingoists who might brand him "soft on Communism" were he to back away from the challenge in Vietnam. So, politician that he was, he assuaged the brass and the braid with promises he may have never intended to keep. At a White House reception on Christmas eve 1963, for example, he told the joint chiefs of staff: "Just let me get elected, and then you can have your war."

In short, Karnow attributes to Johnson very much what O'-Donnell attributes to Kennedy; assuage the right, get elected, and then do what you choose. What LBJ chose was to drag his feet much as JFK had done. That is Newman's evidence of the "far-reaching and profound nature of this reversal" that changed the course of history.[41]

Newman concedes that JFK's public statements refute his thesis, but that's easily handled, as we have seen: JFK was cleverly feinting to delude the right by preaching about the high stakes to the general public—who largely didn't care or were uneasy about the war, as JFK and his advisers knew, and could only be aroused to oppose withdrawal by this inflammatory rhetoric.

As for the internal record, it reveals only JFK's advocacy of withdrawal *after* victory is secure, and exhortations to everyone to "focus on winning the war." It reveals further that the failure of the Diem-Nhu regime to show sufficient enthusiasm for that task was a factor in the effort of JFK and his advisers to overthrow it, only enhanced by the Diem-Nhu gestures towards political settlement and the increasingly insistent calls for US withdrawal. These were regarded as a dangerous threat, not an opportunity to carry out the alleged intent to withdraw. Newman skirts these issues, and nowhere considers their import. Nor does he consider the fact that JFK refused to exploit the high-level military opposition to the war to fend off the jingoist right. The fact that JFK's closest associates either knew nothing about his secret intentions, or were concealing them with remarkable uniformity (pre-Tet, that is), also passes without mention. Nor is there an explanation for the fact that the basic principles of JFK's policies persisted after the assassination, with tactical modifications as dictated by changing assessments, and implemented by Kennedy's most trusted advisers, while the most extreme doves among them lauded LBJ for his "wise caution" in rejecting the twin perils of escalation and withdrawal (Mansfield, Ball).

The withdrawal policy, Newman contends, can be traced to a JFK comment of April 1962 with "profound implications": he told Harriman and Forrestal that "he wished us to be prepared to *seize any favorable moment to reduce our commitment*, recognizing that the moment might yet be some time away" (Newman's emphasis). The "implications" are virtually zero. Note that Newman disagrees with advocates of the withdrawal thesis who trace JFK's secret plans to a post-missile-crisis conversion. The "institutional origin" of JFK's secret withdrawal plan came in May 1962, Newman continues, when McNamara ordered General Harkins to initiate plans to turn "full responsibility over to South Vietnam" and to reduce the US military command—at a moment of great optimism over the prospects, as Newman fully concedes, thus pulling the rug out from under his thesis.[42]

Newman's efforts to deal with that problem are not easy to unravel. He asserts that the 1962 optimism was generated by conscious "deception *within* deception" by MACV. The military knew the reports of progress were false, he claims, and were spinning "webs of deception" to hide the failure of the war effort from McNamara and the President. Evidence for all of this is zero.

Newman's claim requires some interesting assumptions, given the internal record surveyed earlier. Not only must MACV have been lying to McNamara and JFK, but the military were lying to one another from field officers on up, everyone was lying to the CIA who were lying to everyone else, State was in on it, and so on. Discipline has been so remarkable that no trace of this huge "web of deception" appears in the record, and in 30 years no credible voice has come forth to expose any part of it; unusual, to say the least. We also have to assume extraordinary stupidity on the part of the Secretary of Defense, the Director of the CIA, the head of State Department intelligence, and other top advisers of the President—who, alone, "must have known" the truth "in his heart." Newman finds the optimistic projections by Harkins inexplicable (288), implying perhaps (it is hard to be sure) that Harkins was somewhere within the webs of deception. He ignores the explanation given by Krepinich, the military historian on whom he relies throughout. Given the plausibility of Krepinich's explanation, Newman's theory of the evil military command conspiring to deceive the isolated peacenik at the helm also fades away—not to speak of the views of the military, which he never examines (see chapter 1.13).

Though JFK allegedly put his secret plan in motion in early 1962, as of August 26, 1963, Newman reports, "the most basic questions remained unanswered," specifically, whether to "move our resources out or to move our troops in" (Rusk) if the plans to overthrow the Diem-Nhu regime fail. The alternatives, Newman observes, were stark: "withdrawal while losing or massive American intervention." The choice was not made at the August 26 meeting, or even discussed. JFK raised a few questions, nothing more. What "irresistibly impressed itself on the President," Newman states, was "whether the coup was necessary to win the war." In short, victory remained the condition for withdrawal.

Newman does not report the follow-up meeting on August 28, at which JFK gave his usual answer to the "most basic question." Rejecting both horns of Newman's stark dilemma, JFK urged that everything should be done in Washington and Vietnam to "maximize the chances of the rebel generals" to overthrow the regime. The reason was that without a coup, we "must withdraw" and "cannot win the war" (JFK, Harriman, Hilsman)—an unacceptable option for the President and his dovish advisers.[43]

We have now reached the end of August, 1963, with evidence for JFK's secret plan nonexistent. Continuing, we find that as of October 2, when the McNamara-Taylor withdrawal recommendations were presented, "So far, it had been couched in terms of battlefield success. "It was not until after the November 1 coup that the truth filtered to the top, with a "sudden turnabout of reporting in early November." "As the Honolulu meeting approached the tide turned toward pessimism as suddenly and as swiftly as the optimistic interlude had begun in early 1962," Newman writes. The participants in the November 20 meeting received "shocking military news." "The upshot of the Honolulu meeting," he continues, "was that the shocking deterioration of the war effort was presented in detail to those assembled, along with a plan to widen the war, while the 1,000-man withdrawal was turned into a meaningless paper drill." The fact that prior to the "sudden turn toward pessimism" the entire discussion of withdrawal had been "couched in terms of battlefield success" thoroughly undermines Newman's thesis, as becomes only more clear if we introduce the internal record that he ignores.[44]

The way Newman handles these problems is again instructive. Instead of drawing the obvious conclusions, he marvels at "the irony of the elaborate deception story, begun in early 1962," "originally designed" by the military to "forestall Kennedy from a precipitous withdrawal," then reversed by JFK, "judo style—to justify just that." JFK's plan was "brilliant," "duplicitous," "imaginative"; to be more accurate, imaginary, since not a particle of evidence has been offered. As the slender case disappears into the mist, we find that O'Donnell's memoir and a few similar post-Tet recollections come to be the definitive evidence that JFK intended to withdraw. That he intended to withdraw *without victory* is proven by his secret thoughts. LBJ's sordid plots are demonstrated in the manner reviewed. The facts now readily fall into place, whatever they may be: they simply illustrate layer upon layer of intrigue and deception.

A few examples illustrate: "what is particularly striking about Kennedy's behavior is the length to which he went to disguise his intent, and the way in which he used the story of success—a fiction for which he had been the target—against its perpetra-

tors"; "we already know that Kennedy planned to withdraw grad-
ually..." and that his public pose was deception, knowledge
granted to us by stipulation; JFK's strident public call for victory
and against withdrawal only "highlights the desperation of his
dilemma and the poignancy of that moment," as he tries to "erect
[an] alibi" for his plans, secret from everyone, including his top
advisers and closest associates. And so on.

We then wander further along paths "shrouded in mystery
and intrigue," guided by confident assertions about what various
participants "knew," "pretended," "felt," "intended," etc. The facts,
whatever they may be, are interpreted so as to conform to the
central dogma. Given the rules of the game (deceit, hidden intent, etc.), there can be no counter-argument: evidence refuting
the thesis merely shows the depths of the mystery and intrigue.[45]

Newman discusses the McNamara-Taylor withdrawal proposal, the November 20 Honolulu conference, and the first Johnson document (NSAM 273). Putting aside hidden "intents,"
"realizations," "apparent feelings," "webs of deception," etc., his
account adds little to the record already reviewed from the *Pentagon Papers* and the official history, and is factually inaccurate.[46] I
will not pursue the convoluted interpretations—in particular, his
effort to find a "significant" difference between the draft of NSAM
273 and the final version, which falls apart when one examines the
record, already reviewed. Nothing lurks beneath the shrouds.

Newman's media role is hardly more impressive. Responding
to critics of the movie *JFK* in the *New York Times*, he claims that
"Kennedy's public comments in 1963 are sharply contradicted by
his private ones," which is false, if "private ones" are taken to be
those in the internal documentary record, not just the post-Tet
reconstructions. He writes that "Recently declassified documents
reveal" that Kennedy was "privy to intelligence that exposed optimism about the war to be unfounded." That could be true, as it
certainly is true for Kennedy's advisers. The question is whether

anyone accepted these more pessimistic reports, and if so, why they continued to profess optimism in internal discussion; why, as Newman puts it, everything was "couched in terms of battlefield success" until the "shocking" revelations after the November 1963 coup. But whether true or not, the statement is irrelevant without evidence that JFK understood what all of his associates failed to see. None appears in the book, beyond mystic insight.[47]

In a *Boston Globe* op-ed, Newman denounces George Lardner of the *Washington Post*, who wrote that NSAM 273 continued JFK's withdrawal policy. Sneering at this "irresponsible journalistic fiction" and "journalistic license," Newman writes that NSAM 273 only referred to "a slippery White House statement of October 3, 1963," which conditioned withdrawal on military progress, and "failed to address the 1,000 man withdrawal specifically or Kennedy's top secret order—NSAM-263—of October 11, 1963, which implemented it." In reality, NSAM 263 referred to (and can charitably be taken as calling for) the implementation of the military recommendations of the McNamara-Taylor report of October 2, all conditioned on victory. NSAM 273 refers to the White House statement of October 2 (not October 3), already cited, which approves the very same proposal. Furthermore, NSAM 273 is identical to the draft prepared for Kennedy in this respect. In his book, going beyond the evidence, Newman writes that in NSAM 263, "Kennedy actually implemented the [McNamara-Taylor] plan, directing that 1,000 men be withdrawn before the end of the year." But, Newman adds correctly, the condition was "that 'no further reductions in U.S. strength would be made until the requirements of the 1964 [military] campaigns were clear'." His accurate statement that, "So far, it had been couched in terms of battlefield success," adequately refutes his own claims in the denunciation of "journalistic license."

Continuing the denunciation, Newman claims again that "Kennedy's public statements contradicted his private ones," citing only the alleged statements to Congressmen and to O'Donnell, which, Newman asserts, made his intent to withdraw "abundantly clear." Newman falsely claims that the secret record "is more explicit," citing NSAM 263, which "seems to buttress the case that Kennedy was feinting right while moving left," which it surely does not. He also makes the remarkable claim that in 1961 Kennedy rejected the dispatch of combat troops to Vietnam "when all the arguments that could be mustered for sending them had been made—the same arguments, incidentally, which led Johnson to approve sending combat troops in 1965." The conditions were so radically different that the comparison is meaningless; no one would claim that escalation on the scale of JFK's 1961-1962 moves would have sufficed for military victory in 1965.

In a lengthy response to a detailed and accurate exposure by Alexander Cockburn of his misrepresentation of documentary evidence, Newman evades the factual issues raised entirely, preferring supercilious dismissal of this "loose cannon" who "knows little about this subject" and therefore "has distinguished himself by poking fun at serious scholars" with "ad hominem" charges: "it is time to stop joking around and get serious." We find the same appeal to the "top-secret documentary record" and to JFK's alleged knowledge that "the war was a lost cause." Cockburn is advised "to hit the books for a while" and study the documents. Perhaps he would do better to study with a good psychic, so he too might see into JFK's heart.[48]

The hero-villain scenario, and the dual theses on which it rests, are by no means definitively refuted, nor could they be; but Newman's efforts diminish their plausibility still further. His injunction "to hit the books for a while" is well taken. When we follow it, we find that his theses are undermined at every turn. The primary value of his contribution is to reveal the extraordinary lengths to which it is necessary to go to try to make a case for the theses advanced by Newman, Schlesinger, and a wide range of others.

Whatever genre this may be, concern for fact has been left far behind. As in the case of the post-Tet memoirs, this strange performance and its reception are of some interest, but not as a contribution to history; rather, as a chapter of cultural history in the late 20th century.

Perhaps a few words might be added on the latest episode, the publication of a book by the man who served as the model for Oliver Stone's "Deep Throat," the all-knowing "Man X" of his movie *JFK*, whose work "provided vital parts of the movie's theme."[49] The author, Fletcher Prouty, has long been a central figure in the theories of a "secret team" that has hijacked the state, "the crime of the century" being only one feat. He shows, Stone writes in his introduction, that the CIA killed John F. Kennedy because he was withdrawing from Vietnam, failing to pursue the Cuba adventure with sufficient vigor, and "fundamentally...affecting the economic might of this nation-planet, U.S.A., Inc., and its New World Order"; also undermining the Federal Reserve Board, "The CIA and its thousand-headed Medusa of an economic system," and the entire global order run by the "High Cabal" that rules the world. For this achievement, Prouty's "name will go down in history."

Kennedy's October 1963 withdrawal plan was "a seismic change that would have defused the Cold War," Prouty writes, a consequence intolerable to the High Cabal, a global "super power elite" that bases its thinking on "a quartet of the greatest propaganda schemes ever put forth by man": Locke's philosophy of natural law, the population theory of Malthus, Darwin's theory of evolution, and Heisenberg's theory of indeterminacy, a collection of "errors and confusion" that underlie the "invisible war" called the Cold War. The Cabal had already selected Vietnam as a "major battleground" during World War II, when they shipped stockpiles intended for the invasion of Japan to Vietnam, turning them over to Ho Chi Minh and his top commander Vo Nguyen

Giap. "Decisions of such magnitude" could only have been made by a "super power elite" standing above such figures as FDR, Churchill, Stalin, and other official leaders. He suggests Averell Harriman as the closest model.

The entire game was to be ended by JFK, the "bombshell" being NSAM 263, a document so extraordinary that "many historians and journalists" deny its existence, and the record leading to it "has been savagely distorted in basic government documents," including "such grandiose 'cover story' creations as the *Pentagon Papers*," with its "subtle anti-Kennedy slant" and selection of documents that is "the source of the anti-Kennedy forgeries." The State Department history, reviewed earlier, is a complex effort "to further obfuscate this record" in order to maintain "the cover story"; the proof is that documents are presented in chronological order (as always in these publications), requiring the reader to cross-check (following the precise instructions given). NSAM 273 was "a total reversal of Kennedy's own policy." Many other events of the past half-century have been "caused to happen" in accord with the "game plan of the High Cabal," Prouty relates.

Apart from some phrases from the documentary record, the evidence is anecdotal, based on the author's alleged direct participation in these awesome events.

Again, questions of contemporary cultural history arise, but little more.

4. Kennedy and the Political Norm

A methodological point is perhaps worth mention. Suppose that we were to concoct a theory about historical events at random, while permitting ourselves to assume arbitrary forms of deceit and falsification. Then in the vast documentary record, we are sure to find scattered hints and other debris that could be made to conform to the theory, while counter-evidence is nullified. By that method, one can "prove" virtually anything. For example, we can prove that JFK never intended to withdraw any troops, citing the elusiveness of NSAM 263 and his unwillingness to commit himself to the withdrawal recommended by his war managers. Or we can prove that the attempt to assassinate Reagan was carried out by dark forces (Alexander Haig, the CIA, etc.). After all, Reagan had backed away from using US forces directly in Central America (unlike JFK in Vietnam); he was cozying up to the Chicoms; he had already given intimations of the anti-nuclear passion that led him to offer to give away the store at Rejkjavik and to join forces with the arch-fiend Gorbachev, whose *perestroika* was a transparent plot to entrap us; his associates were planning off-the-shelf international operations, bypassing intelligence and the Pentagon. Obviously, he has to go. Or suppose there had been an attempt to assassinate LBJ in late 1964, when he was refusing the call of the military to stand up to the Commies in Vietnam, pursuing Great Society and civil rights programs with a zeal well beyond Kennedy, and about to defeat a real alternative, Barry Goldwater. Nothing is easier than to construct a high-level conspiracy to get rid of this "radical reformer." The task is only facilitated by a search for nuances and variations of phrasing in the mountains of documents, usually committee jobs put together hastily with many compromises.

This is not the way to learn about the world. In particular, the widespread belief that JFK was a secret dove has to be explained on some grounds other than his position on Vietnam.

Are there other grounds? Another favored idea is that JFK had become a demon to the military-industrial complex because he was going to end the Cold War. To assess the thesis, we may turn again to the speech he was to give in Dallas on the day of the assassination, with its proud boast about his vast increases in Polaris submarines, Minuteman missiles, strategic bombers on 15-minute alert, nuclear weapons in strategic alert forces,

readiness of conventional forces, procurement, naval construc-
tion and modernization, tactical aircraft, and special forces. JFK
military Keynesianism had raised Pentagon spending from $45.3
billion in 1960 to $52.1 billion in 1962, along with a huge in-
crease in the space budget from $400 million in 1960 to $5 billion in 1965, much of it for the jingoist "man-on-the-moon"
extravaganza. By the end of JFK's term, over 78 percent of all
R&D was funded by the federal government, overwhelmingly
military and space (barely distinguishable), almost all for the "private sector," a huge increase in three years. Recall further that
all of this had been achieved on the pretext of a fabricated missile
gap and other fantasies about how Eisenhower was "frittering
away" our wealth in "indulgences, luxuries, and frivolities" while
the country faced "the possibility of annihilation or humiliation"
(senior Kennedy economic adviser Walter Heller). At Dallas,
JFK intended to call for more of the same, because "we dare not
weary of the task" of confronting "the ambitions of international
communism," his "monolithic and ruthless conspiracy."[50] Reagan
could hardly claim more.

Perhaps the Dallas speech can be explained away by the "delude the right" gambit. More imagination would be required to
deal with some facts that JFK did not intend to share with his
audience: namely, his knowledge that Soviet Premier Nikita
Khrushchev had undertaken huge cuts in active Soviet military
forces, verified by US intelligence, including elimination of half
the tactical air force (with two-thirds reduction in light-bomber
units) and removal of about 1,500 aircraft from the Navy, half
of them scrapped and the rest turned over to air defense; that
Khrushchev had withdrawn more than 15,000 troops from East
Germany, calling on the US to undertake similar reductions of
the military budget and in military forces in Europe and generally; and that in 1963 Khrushchev had proposed further recipro-
cal cuts—options privately discussed by Kennedy with high

Soviet officials, but dismissed by the President as he expanded his intervention in Vietnam.[51]

This does not seem too promising a path.

The 1963 Limited Test Ban Treaty (LTBT) is regularly invoked in this connection. On its import, we may turn to McGeorge Bundy, hardly one given to downplay the achievements of the Kennedy Administration, or its peaceful intent. The LTBT "was indeed limited," he writes, and did not impede the technological advance in nuclear weaponry, which is what was important to US strategic planners. Bundy agrees with Glenn Seaborg, chairman of the Atomic Energy Commission under Kennedy and Johnson, that "what produced the treaty was steadily growing worldwide concern over the radioactive fallout from testing," along with Kennedy's ability to show "moderation" after facing down Khrushchev at the missile crisis, and the latter's interest in appearing to be "on the same level" as the US after that demonstration of Soviet weakness. The same show of strength enabled JFK to deliver a "peace speech" in 1963, Bundy observes.[52]

It also set off the next phase of the arms race, as the USSR tried to compensate for the weakness that had been exposed by JFK's military build-up and uncompromising public posture, which helped bring the world all too close to nuclear war.

Another common belief is that JFK was so incensed over the failure of the CIA at the Bay of Pigs that he vowed to smash it to bits, sowing the seeds for right-wing hatreds. Again, there are problems. As historians of the Agency have pointed out, it was Lyndon Johnson who treated the CIA "with contempt," while JFK's distress over the Bay of Pigs "in no way undermined his firm faith in the principle of covert operations, and in the CIA's mission to carry them out." JFK promised to "redouble his efforts" and to "improve" covert operations. He fired the CIA's harshest critic (Chester Bowles) and appointed as Director the respected John McCone, who "revitalized the intelligence

process," though persistent failures kept the Agency from returning to the "golden age." Nevertheless, the CIA was "reestab-
lished...in White House favor" and became a "significant voice
in policy making" under Kennedy, particularly in 1963, "as covert
actions multiplied in Cuba, Laos, Vietnam and Africa" (including
new instructions in June 1963 to increase covert operations
against Castro). Under JFK, the CIA Director became "a principal participant in the administration, on a par with the Secretary of State or of Defense." The enthusiasm of the Kennedy
brothers for counterinsurgency and covert operations is, of
course, notorious.[53]

Roger Hilsman, Director of State Department Intelligence
under Kennedy, writes of the efforts of the Administration to
streamline intelligence operations and make them more "effective
and appropriate," overcoming the incompetence of recent operations so that later ones would better serve US interests. The intent
is well illustrated by Hilsman's discussion of CIA Director Allen
Dulles's defense of the successful overthrow of the governments
of Iran (Mossadegh) and Guatemala (Arbenz). "Dulles is fundamentally right," Hilsman states. If the Communists remain "an-
tagonistic" and use subversion, then we have a right "to protect
and defend ourselves"—by overthrowing a conservative parliamen-
tary regime or a reformist democratic capitalist government and
imposing a murderous terror state.[54]

Furthermore, as Robert Spears points out, those most incensed by JFK's efforts to improve the efficiency of the CIA after
the Bay of Pigs fiasco were not right-wing jingoists, but the "Bold
Easterners," a group not unlike the "action intellectuals" of the
New Frontier. The "decline in the reputation and standing of the
CIA" paralleled the "decline in the abundance and power of the
Ivy Leaguers." LBJ reduced their role in the decision-making
process, and Nixon "consciously sought to exclude the CIA from
power" because of his contempt for the "Ivy League liberals" who

still dominated the Agency, he felt. The Nixon years were "the nadir for the CIA."[55]

Johnson and Nixon, then, should have been the targets for CIA resentment and plots, not JFK. There seems to be little promise here.

Others have argued that Kennedy's threat was to the business elite and the wealthy, a position hard to square with fiscal policies that overwhelmingly benefited higher income groups, according to an analysis in the *National Tax Journal*, including the 1962 investment credit ("a bribe to capital formation," in Paul Samuelson's phrase) and the Revenue Act of 1964 proposed by Kennedy just before his assassination, which "provided for regressive personal and corporate income tax cuts," economists Du Boff and Herman observe. Note also that no policies relevant to the various theories about Kennedy-the-reformer were reversed under LBJ; those most opposed by the right were extended.[56]

Some have brought forth Latin America as the sign of Kennedy's incipient radicalism. Cuba poses a certain problem for that thesis, notably Kennedy's terrorist war after the Bay of Pigs, which broke entirely new grounds in international terrorism. The threat of invasion it posed also appears to have been a significant factor contributing to the missile crisis. It is often alleged that Kennedy helped end the crisis by committing the US not to invade Cuba. That is not true, Raymond Garthoff pointed out in his authoritative insider's account. There was no such commitment, public or private; the "studied silence" on the matter was "a considered position maintained throughout the Kennedy and Johnson administrations," to be ended in August 1970, "when for the first time American leaders unequivocally accepted the mutual commitments" of 1962. After the crisis ended, Kennedy initiated a new sabotage and terror program, and still sought to "dig Castro out of there" (memorandum of private conversation, March 1963). US-based terrorist operations continued until the assassination, according to reports from the FBI, which monitored them; though "with the assassination,...the heart went out of the offensive," Michael McClintock observes, and the operations were terminated in April 1964 by LBJ, who regarded them as "a damned Murder, Inc. in the Caribbean."[57]

One of the most significant legacies left by the Administration was its 1962 decision to shift the mission of the Latin American military from "hemispheric defense" to "internal security," while providing the means and training to ensure that the task would be properly performed. As described by Charles Maechling, who led counterinsurgency and internal defense planning from 1961 to 1966, that historic decision led to a change from toleration "of the rapacity and cruelty of the Latin American military" to "direct complicity" in "the methods of Heinrich Himmler's extermination squads." The aftermath is well known, including the establishment of the death squads of Central America; the meeting of Central American presidents in March 1963, chaired by JFK, was "the landmark event in the formation of the national security apparatus" in the region, Alan Nairn comments.

These improved modes of repression were a central component of Kennedy's Latin American policies, a companion to the Alliance for Progress, which required effective population control because of the dire impact of its development programs on much of the population. Related projects helped subvert democracy and bring on brutally repressive regimes in El Salvador, the Dominican Republic, Guatemala, British Guiana, Chile, Brazil, and elsewhere. The export-promotion policies of the Alliance brought about comforting "economic miracles" in the technical sense. Unemployment increased from 18 to 25 million and agricultural production per person declined during the "decade of development." The "economic miracles" turned into the crisis of the '70s, setting the stage for vastly increased US-backed terror and forecasts of new "economic miracles" as the old policies are reinstated. Six military coups overthrew popular regimes during the Kennedy years, ten more later; in several cases, Kennedy Administration policies contributed materially to the outcome. In 1962-1963, Kennedy's CIA initiated its (successful) program to subvert the 1964 election in Chile, because, as the NSC determined, "We are not prepared to risk a Socialist or FRAP [Allende] victory, for fear of national-ization of U.S. investments" and "probable Communist influence." The role of the Kennedy Administration in bringing about the Brazilian military coup of 1964 was still more significant.

Putting aside the catastrophic investor-oriented economic policies, there is no serious question that "Through its recognition policy, internal security initiatives, and military and economic aid programs, the [Kennedy] Administration demonstrably bolstered regimes and groups that were undemocratic, conservative, and fre-quently repressive. The short-term security that anti-communist elites could provide was purchased at the expense of long-term political and social democracy" (Stephen Rabe).[58]

Without proceeding any further, it is not easy to make a case that JFK represented some departure from the norm of business rule.

In fact, there are striking resemblances between the Kennedy and Reagan Administrations. Both came into office with impas-sioned denunciations of the wimps in power, who were presiding over America's decline while the Evil Empire pursued its implaca-ble course towards world conquest. Both were "full of belliger-ence," "sort of looking for a chance to prove their muscle" (Chester Bowles on JFK); they warned the country that "the com-placent and the self-indulgent, the soft societies are about to be swept away with the debris of history. Only the strong...can pos-sibly survive" (JFK). Both were enthusiastic innovators in the art of international terrorism and state terror. Both launched huge military build-ups on fraudulent pretexts, with the traditional twin aims of using their muscle abroad and extending the taxpayer

subsidy to high-tech industry. Both initiated regressive fiscal programs for the benefit of investors. In both cases, corporate and
financial sectors called for limits on these Keynesian excesses;
rhetoric became more muted and conciliatory and military
spending levelled (though in the Kennedy-Johnson case, Vietnam intervened).

There were also differences. In the early '60s, the US remained the world's dominant power, and could afford to flaunt
prospects of "great societies at home and grand designs abroad"
(Walter Heller); 20 years later, the great societies would have to
go. Kennedy made a play for the intellectual community, whom
Reagan treated with contempt. The imagery, accordingly, is
much different; the reality, less so.[59]

It seems more than coincidental that fascination with tales
of intrigue about Camelot lost reached their peak in 1992 just as
discontent with all institutions reached historic peaks, along with
a general sense of powerlessness and gloom about the future, and
the traditional one-party, two-faction candidate-producing mech-
anism was challenged by a billionaire with a dubious past, a
"blank slate" on which one's favorite dreams could be inscribed.
The audiences differ, but the JFK-Perot movements share a mil-
lenarian cast, reminiscent of the cargo cults of South Sea islanders
who await the return of the great ships with their bounty. These
developments tell us a good bit about the state of American culture at a time of general malaise, unfocused anger and discontent,
and effective dissolution of the means for the public to become
engaged in a constructive way in determining their fate.[60]

Notes

Notes to the Preface to the 2015 Edition

1. Chomsky, *For Reasons of State*, Pantheon, 1973.
2. Marc Selverstone, "It's a Date: Kennedy and the Timetable for a Vietnam Troop Withdrawal," *Diplomatic History* 34.3, June 2010.
3. See N. Chomsky, "Murdering History," in *Year 501: The Conquest Continues*, South End, 1993.
4. See particularly Sheldon Stern, *The Cuban Missile Crisis in American Memory: Myths versus Reality*, Stanford, 2012.
5. John H. Coatsworth, "The Cold War in Central America, 1975–1991," *The Cambridge History of the Cold War*, vol. III, 2010.

Notes to the Introduction

1. See *501* for much further discussion and sources. Also *DD*, and earlier work cited there.
2. On the media from 1950 through 1985, see *MC* and sources cited. On developments reviewed below, see my books cited in *501*, and sources cited.
3. Kiernan, *Lords*, 15-6. *501*, ch. 1.
4. See particularly Drinnon, *Facing West*. Knox cited by Horsman, *Expansion*, 64.
5. *Ibid.* 122, 64. On the Cherokees, see *501*, ch. 9.3. Weeks, *JQA*, 193.
6. *Ibid.*, ch. 5.
7. For numerous examples, see *TTT*, chapter 3.9, and *501*, chapters 1, 9, among many other sources. The Bush spectacle was presented with proper awe on network TV (Peter Jennings, ABC 7PM, Jan. 5), but kept from the Newspaper of Record (*NYT*, Jan. 6, 1993). To plumb the depths, however, one must look elsewhere, for example, to the gushing tribute to colonialist atrocities ("colonialism is an act of generosity and idealism of which only rising civilizations are capable," etc.) by Angelo

185

Codevilla of Stanford University's Hoover Institute (*Wall Street Journal*, Jan. 7, 1993). For similar effusions in the British press, see my Raymond Williams memorial lecture, London, Nov. 1992. In a seminar at MIT, US Census Bureau specialist Beth Daponte estimated 111,000 civilian casualties from the effects of the Gulf war (AP, AFP, *Age*, Australia, Sept. 10, 1992). In *Figaro* (Paris), Claude Lorieux reports from Iraq that the worst suffering from the embargo is among the Shi'ites in the South, citing UNICEF figures (*World Press Review*, Jan. 1993). A Harvard Study Team estimated that 50,000 children died in the first eight months of 1991, many from the effects of radioactive artillery shells (Eric Hoskins, op-ed, *NYT*, Jan. 21, 1993, a rare mention of the ongoing disaster).

8.   Friedman, *NYT*, Jan. 12, 1992; Horsman, *Expansion*, 15f.
9.   Frederick Starr, *NYT Book Review*, July 19, 1992.
10. James Morgan, lead article, *Weekend FT, Financial Times* (London), April 25/26, 1992.
11. See Simpson, *Splendid*, for a comprehensive review for Germany. On the parallel accomplishments elsewhere, see *DD*, ch. 10.
12. Daly and Goodland, "An Ecological-Economic Assessment of Deregulation of International Commerce Under GATT," Draft, Environment Department, World Bank, 1992.
13. In addition to references of note 1, see Edward Herman, "Doublespeak," *Z magazine*, Nov. 1992, and my "'Mandate for Change,' or Business as Usual," Z, Feb. 1993.
14. See *FRS*, ch. l.V (reprinted in Peck, *Chomsky Reader*). *501*, ch. 5, on the reaction to the 1965 Indonesia bloodbath. See *PEHR*, vol. I, on the general pattern.
15. Lars-Erik Nelson, "Bush's wise counsel on the use of force," *Boston Globe*, Jan. 9, 1993.
16. For details, see *FRS*, ch. 1. V (Peck, *op.cit.*).
17. *Ibid.*
18. Editorial, *WP*, Nov. 20, 1991.
19. Kennan, *Russia*, 352-63.
20. *DD*, ch. 1.4. Simpson, *Splendid*, ch. 5. Yergin, *Shattered Peace*, 24-26. Nolte cited by Thomas Sheehan, *NY Review*, Jan. 14, 1993.
21. *FRUSV*, I, 343; III, 4n. Gibbons, *US Government*, 70-1, citing Air Force history.
22. Americas Watch, *Political Murder and Reform in Colombia: the Violence Continues* (New York, 1992), citing State Department *Country Reports*, 1990, and House Committee on Government Operations, *Stopping the Flood of Cocaine with Operation Snowcap: Is it Working?*, Aug. 14, 1990, pp. 83-4. Jorge Gómez Lizarro, human rights activist and former Judge, "Colombian Blood, U.S. Guns," *NYT*, Op-Ed, Jan. 28, 1992.
23. *Colombia Update* 1.4, Dec. 1989. *DD*, *501*, for further discussion.
24. Westing, *Herbicides*, 22. Vo Quy, *Third World Resurgence* (Penang,

Malaysia), No. 26, 1992.

25. Weeks, *op.cit.*

26. For a few examples, see *MC*, ch. 5.5.2 and App. 3; *NI*, App. I.2; *LL*, letter 18. See p. 142 below.

27. Nayan Chanda, *Far Eastern Economic Review*, Dec. 17, 1992. A Thai intelligence report estimates that the projected cash flow "dwarfs the combined revenues of the three other factions, and could become a decisive factor in the power struggle" that may restore the Thai-backed Khmer Rouge to power. Ken Stier, *FEER*, Jan. 21, 1993.

28. See *PEHR*, vol. II, 35ff.

29. Shenon, *NYT*, Dec. 26, 1992; *FEER*, Jan. 7, 1993; Victor Mallet, *FT*, Dec. 16, 1992.

30. Holmes, *NYT*, Dec. 15; Constable, *BG*, Nov. 22; Shenon, Nov. 30, 1992.

31. *NYT*, Oct. 24, 1992.

32. *PP*. The Department of Defense later released an edition with additional materials. For extensive material from both, and discussion, see *FRS*. U.S. Dept. of State, *FRUSV*, I-III; *FRUSV-64* (1964 is the latest volume released). For a brief and accurate summary of the 1963, 1964 volumes, see *Economist*, Jan. 18, May 16, 1992. Another useful source is Gibbons, *US Government*.

33. Sources already cited, and others in the dissident literature, gave a generally accurate picture as events proceeded, requiring little modification in the light of what is now known. For a summary, see *MC*. The following summary is largely extracted from *501*, ch. 10.8.

34. See *501*, ch. 2.4.

35. On this matter, see particularly Kahin, *Intervention*.

36. On the complicity of the intellectual community in suppressing the readily-available facts about US subversion of diplomacy, see *TCNW*, ch. 3; *MC*, ch. 5.5.3. Parts of the story are yet untold.

37. *AWWA*, 286.

38. For a (very small) sample, see *Tikkun*, March/April 1992; Pete Karman, *In These Times*, March 11, 1992; letters, *Nation*, March 9, 1992, and an enormous number of similar letters not published, responding angrily to Alexander Cockburn's questioning of these beliefs; Michael Parenti, *Z magazine*, Jan. 1993. Also much discussion on community-based radio, in movement journals, correspondence, and other channels out of the mainstream. See also next chapter, p. 106. For some early criticism of these tendencies, see *I.F. Stone's Weekly*, "The Left and the Warren Commission Report," Oct. 5, 1964.

Notes to Chapter 1

1. Leffler, *Preponderance*, 166, 258. *FRS*, 32-3. See *501*, ch. 2.1-2.

2. Leffler, 334, 463, 17, 339; also 468f. Cumings, *Origins*, 57. See references

of *501*, ch. 2, n. 16.

3. *PP*, I 597, 434f. *AWWA*, 33f.
4. *FRS*, 100ff.; Kahin, *Intervention*, 74.
5. *FRS*, ch. 1.6; 72-3; reprinted in Peck, *Chomsky Reader*. Also *APNM*, 59, for more on "internal aggression."
6. *FRUSV-64*, 158.
7. Oct. 31, 1964; *ibid.*, 864ff.
8. Among others, see Kahin, *Intervention;* Kinnard, *War Managers*, 37. Koreans, *PEHR*, I, 5.1.4. Roger Hilsman, Director of State Department intelligence and later Assistant Secretary for Far Eastern Affairs under the Kennedy Administration and for some months after the assassination, alleged in 1967 that "later evidence" shows the presence of at least one battalion of North Vietnamese regulars by the time of the February 1965 bombing of the South (which might bring them up to the level of the US Korean mercenaries), but "that *the United States did not know of this fact at that time*" (his emphasis); Hilsman, *To Move a Nation*, 531n.
9. *FRUSV-64*, 234-5; report of conversation; *"sic"* is in the source text. On de Gaulle and Europe, see *501*, ch. 2.3.
10. Lodge, *PP*, II 304; *FRUSV-64*, 18. See *MC*, ch. 5, for review.
11. *PP*, III 526; *FRUSV-64*, 676. Bundy was a high Pentagon official under JFK and LBJ, then Assistant Secretary of State for Far Eastern Affairs.
12. See *NI* and *DD* (including 1992 "Afterword") for recent examples, review, and sources. Michael Gordon, *NYT*, Jan. 8, 1993.
13. JFK, "America's Stake in Vietnam," American Friends of Vietnam Symposium, 1956, cited by Chester Cooper, *Lost Crusade*, 168.
14. Kennedy address to UN General Assembly, Sept. 25, 1961, cited in Gaddis, *Strategies*, 208; *PP*, II 824, 828f.; Schlesinger, *1000 Days*, 902; *FRUSV*, IV 94; Newman, *JFK and Vietnam*, 387; Hilsman, *To Move a Nation*, 505-6. Cuba, see *501*, 146.
15. Newman, *JFK and Vietnam*, 323, 425-7, 457; *PP*, II 817, 831; Paterson, *Kennedy's Quest*, 20-1, 248ff.
16. See secs. 6-7. *FRUSV-64* 154. Schlesinger, *RFK*, 728, 730. Sorenson, *Kennedy Legacy*, 214.
17. Bundy, cited by David Fromkin and James Chace, *Foreign Affairs* (Spring 1985). See *FRS*, 48f., and much subsequent discussion, including *PEHR* and *MC*.
18. IDA study on pacification by Chester Cooper, et al., cited by Bergerud, *Dynamics*, 14; Kolko, *Anatomy*, 89, giving the "conservative estimate" of 12,000 killed for 1955-57; Fall, *New Society*, April 22, 1965; reprinted in Fall and Raskin, *Vietnam Reader*. The US Government accepted the 89,000 figure; see minutes of July 1965 meetings cited by Kahin, *Intervention*, 385.
19. Bergerud, *Dynamics*, 13f., 18f., 47. *PP*, II 134. See sec. 3, below. On Laos, see *AWWA*, *FRS*, and sources cited.
20. *PP*, II 360, 656-8, 677. Newman, *JFK and Vietnam*, 205-6. Crop de-

struction, Kahin, *Intervention*, 478.

21. Hilsman, *To Move a Nation*, 444, 442. Operations against North, see below. Bergerud, *Dynamics*, 256, 70. For some details on the early stages of JFK's aggression and the "accidental" atrocities, along with a tortured effort to depict the President's initiatives as opposition to escalation, see Newman, *JFK and Vietnam*, 149ff., 159ff., 201ff.

22. *PP*, II 455, 706-9, 714, 696, 703, 717-18. *FRUSV*, III 51, 57. Duncanson, *Government and Revolution*, 321. On Cambodia, see particularly Ben Kiernan, "The American Bombardment of Kampuchea, 1969-1973," *Vietnam Generation*, 1.1 (1989).

23. *FRS*, 141.

24. *NYT*, March 10; AP, *NYT*, Oct 17, p. 1; Oct. 22, 1962. David Halberstam, *NYT*, Oct. 16, 1962; Shaplen, *Lost Revolution*, 170ff.

25. Tregaskis, *Vietnam Diary*, 108; Browne, *New Face of War*, 118.

26. Hilsman, *To Move a Nation*, 437-56, 524; "Two American Counterstrategies to Guerrilla Warfare," in Tsou, *China*. *PP*, II 149, 130. See *FRS*, ch. 1.VI.5.2, for more on the concept of "democracy" and "free choice" as understood by the planners.

27. Lewy, *America in Vietnam*, 24f.; *TNCW*, 404-5. On the Nazi model for counterinsurgency, see McClintock, Instruments, 58ff., 207ff. *501*, ch. 10.3.

28. For review, see *FRS*, ch. 1.VI.1. Fall, *New Republic*, Oct. 9, 1965.

29. Race, *War;* Bergerud, *Dilemmas*. I am personally indebted to Race for having shared some of his material with me in the late 1960s. Though I could not cite it before publication, it influenced my own understanding of the war.

30. Hilsman, *To Move a Nation*, 112. See *AWWA*, ch. 3.

31. Peter Applebome, *NYT*, March 1; Terrence Maitland, *NYT Book Review*, Feb. 3, 1991, reviewing Zalin Grant, *Facing the Phoenix.*

32. John Marciano, "Ideological Hegemony and the War Against Vietnam: A Critique of United States History Textbooks," State U. of NY at Cortland, ms., 1992. See also Griffen and Marciano, *Lessons;* David Berman, "In Cold Blood: Vietnam in Textbooks," *Vietnam Generation* 1.1, 1989.

33. Kamow, *Vietnam*. On its severe factual errors and distortion, see my "Vietnam War in the Age of Orwell," *Race & Class* (London: 4, 1984); *Boston Review*, Jan. 1984. On the patriotic bias of the accompanying TV series, and the intriguing interpretation of it as a left-wing deviation, see *MC*, 248ff.; illustrations throughout of elite opinion and the efforts to bring the public back into line. Opinion surveys, Gallup, for Chicago Council on Foreign Relations (*MC*, 238, on 1982, 1986).

34. For examples, see *LL*, letter 17.

35. Kaplan, *BG*, Feb. 23; Hoffmann, *BG*, Jan. 6, 1991. Sut Jhally, Justin Lewis, & Michael Morgan, *The Gulf War: A Study of the Media, Public Opinion, & Public Knowledge*, Department of Communications, U

Mass. Amherst; Morgan, et al., in Mowlana, *Triumph*.

36. I will use the term, though with a cautionary note, such terms as "left" and "conservative" having been largely deprived of significance, along with much of the terminology of political discourse.

37. The suggestion of a significant change dates to an interesting analysis by Peter Dale Scott in 1972 (*PP* V). Whatever plausibility the idea may then have had, it is not easy to reconcile with the extensive documentation now available.

38. Newman, *JFK and Vietnam;* Stone, *Cineaste,* no. 1, 1992. Zachary Sklar, co-author of the screenplay, also describes Newman's book as "largely what we relied on" (*ibid.*).See also pp. 175-6, below, on Fletcher Prouty. Town Hall Forum, March 3, 1992; William Grimes, *NYT,* March 5, 1992. Michael Specter, "Explosive Imagery of 'JFK' Igniting Debate in Audiences," *NYT,* Dec. 23, 1991. Pfaff, *LA Times* Syndicate, for release Jan. 11/12, 1992. San Diego TV, AP, April 16, 1992. Costner quoted in the *Nation,* Jan. 6, 1992, by Alexander Cockburn, whose criticisms of the film and alleged historical background aroused impassioned denunciation in the left press.

39. Schlesinger, *NYT Book Review,* March 29, 1992. Among others, see Guy Halverson, *Christian Science Monitor,* March 19, 1992.

40. See the introduction, n. 32

41. *PP,* II 174. Schlesinger, *1000 Days,* 506-8, 695.

42. Kinnard, *War Managers,* 128.

43. Zinn, *Vietnam.* Unable to obtain any notice of the book, Zinn asked me to write about it, as I did. See *APNM,* ch. 3.

44. *PP,* II 175ff.; *FRUSV,* III 35ff.

45. *Ibid.,* 73-94, 191-2. Feb. 1 date, 94-5, 97. Forrestal, whose optimism was more qualified than Wheeler's (see below), criticized the latter's "rosy euphoria" to the President (97).

46. Bundy, Jan. 7, 1964; *FRUSV-64,* 4. Forrestal, *FRUSV,* IV 699. Pfaff, *op. cit.*

47. See *AWWA, PEHR, MC.*

48. *FRUSV,* III 49-62.

49. *FRUSV,* III 243-5, 193, 270, 295, 591, 659.

50. *Ibid.,* 246, 223, 294n.

51. *FRUSV,* IV 1ff., 27, 50f., 75-8, 89, 295f., 325. On Hilsman's later interpretation of his Aug. 30 memorandum, see next chapter, n. 21.

52. *Ibid.,* 55n, 81f., 94, 100.

53. *Ibid.,* 171, 177-9, 221ff. Also Gibbons, *US Government,* 177f., with additional detail (and slightly different wording, used here).

54. *FRUSV,* IV 248, 213, 209. For extensive discussion of the concerns in Washington over neutralization and forced withdrawal, see Kahin, *Intervention.*

55. Gibbons, *US Government,* 180f.; *FRUSV,* IV 252f., 278-81.

56. *Ibid.,* 330, 336ff. *PP,* II 751-66; 187, 756.

57. *FRUSV,* IV 350f. *Public Papers of the Presidents,* 1963, 759-60.
58. *FRUSV,* IV 370, 395-6, 371ff.
59. *Ibid.,* 359, 387.
60. *Ibid.,* 385-6, 402. On Indonesia, see *501,* ch. 5, p. 122.
61. *FRUSV,* IV 418-20, 448.
62. *Ibid.,* 472, 579-80.
63. *Ibid.,* 581ff., 592ff.
64. *Ibid.,* 582f., 596, 608ff.
65. Tad Szulc, "Vietnam Victory by the End of '65 Envisaged by U.S.," *NYT,* Oct. 3; transcript of press conference, *NYT,* Nov. 1; Joseph Loftus, *NYT,* Nov. 1. Jack Raymond, *NYT,* Nov. 13; "G.I. Return Waits on Vietnam Talk," Nov. 15, with transcript of News Conference. AP, "1,000 US. Troops to Leave Vietnam," *NYT,* Nov. 16; David Halberstam, *NYT,* Nov. 21; AP, *NYT,* Dec. 2; Hedrick Smith, *NYT,* Dec. 4, 1963.
66. *FRUSV,* IV 637ff. "Draft, National Security Action Memorandum No.," McGeorge Bundy, declassified 1/31/91.
67. *FRUSV-64,* 4-5; Joint Draft plan, the basis for Operations Plan (OPLAN) 34A-64, Jan. 3. *Ibid.,* 28f.
68. See note 38. Schlesinger, "'JFK': Truth and Fiction," *Wall Street Journal,* Jan. 10, 1992. On Schlesinger's efforts to establish the reversal, see ch. 2.2.
69. *PP,* III 668-9.
70. *FRUSV,* IV 695, 710. *PP,* III 242, 237; IV 618.
71. *FRUSV-64,* 401.
72. Ball, *Past,* 366f.; *New York Review,* Feb. 13, 1992 (virtually the same).
73. Newman, *JFK and Vietnam,* 141.
74. *FRUSV,* III 587-8, IV 691-2; *FRUSV-64,* 222f., 1010f. *PP,* III 263. *APNM,* 370-1.
75. Gibbons, *US Government,* 215f.; emphases in original.
76. *FRUSV,* IV 640, 652, 629, 635f.; *FRUSV-64,* 119-20.
77. *FRUSV,* IV 681ff., 698f., 704ff., 722.
78. *Ibid.,* 728-53.
79. *FRUSV-64,* 1ff.
80. *PP,* III 496-9; *FRUSV-64,* 35.
81. *Ibid.,* 120, 129, 167ff.
82. *Ibid.,* 174, 206-7, 387-8, 806.
83. His emphasis. *Ibid.,* 176ff. The quotes in the last sentence appear in an excerpt in Hilsman's memoir *To Move a Nation,* 536, with the word "continue" and a later reference to ongoing operations deleted.
84. *FRUSV-64,* 197-8, 206, 224, 273.
85. *Ibid.,* 374, 387-8, 437f., 475, 598ff.
86. *Ibid.,* 717, 723.
87. *Ibid.,* 742f., 759, 778f., 806, 847, 933, 948f., 1049f., 1057f.
88. *Ibid.,* 17-8, 480-1.
89. *Ibid.,* 950-1.

90. Newman, *JFK and Vietnam*, 287-8, 282.
91. Schlesinger, *1000 Days*, 316; *RFK*, 703. Sorenson, *Kennedy*, 641. Raskin, "*JFK* and the Culture of Violence," AHR forum (on the Stone film), *American Historical Review*, April 1992. Buzzanco, "Division, Dilemma and Dissent: Military Recognition of the Peril of War in Vietnam," in Duffy, *Informed Dissent;* "The American Military's Rationale against the Vietnam War," *Political Science Quarterly*, 4, 1986; "Prologue to Tragedy," *Diplomatic History*, forthcoming. VC attitude studies, *APNM*, 243, 282; *FRS*, 5; Anthony Russo, *Ramparts*, April 1972; excerpts from RAND studies, *Ramparts*, Nov. 1972. Raskin adds that Ridgway's successor, Maxwell Taylor, disagreed with Ridgway; Taylor's position "held sway, and it led quickly to dramatic escalations." The latter conclusion is not accurate. Recall that Taylor recommended the October withdrawal plans that *JFK* endorsed with hesitations; see below, on his continued opposition to US combat troops.
92. Buzzanco, "Division, Dilemma, Dissent"; "Waiting for Westy," paper delivered at Conference of Society of Historians of American Foreign Relations, Vassar, June 1992. Reviewing Newman's files, Buzzanco concludes that his work is based on "questionable analysis and uses of sources."
93. Buzzanco, "Division, Dilemma, Dissent." *FRUSV,* IV 170; *FRUSV-64,* 883, 901-2, 909. Berman, *Planning*, 52-6. On Taylor's reluctance, see also Kahin, *Intervention.*
94. *PP,* II 756; III 19 (highlighted), 35f.
95. Buzzanco, "Division, Dilemma, Dissent," "Waiting for Westy," "American Military's Rationale." Bergerud, *Dynamics*, 90.

Notes to Chapter 2

1. Schlesinger, *1000 Days*, 908. The basic point is made accurately by Richard Grenier of the far-right *Washington Times* in the *Times Literary Supplement* (London), letter, March 20, 1992, in response to Schlesinger's Feb. 28 reference to "newly declassified official papers that amply document" Kennedy's "plans for withdrawal," citing Newman. See also the subsequent exchange (Schlesinger, April 3; Grenier, May 1, again accurate).
2. Actually, from 685 when JFK took office to 16,732 in October 1963; Schlesinger, *RFK*, 722.
3. Sorenson, *Kennedy Legacy*, 213-4. Giglio, *Presidency*, 254; Schlesinger, *RFK*, 727, 713, 715, 730, 733-4.
4. Hilsman, *To Move a Nation*, 580, 537, 411.
5. *Ibid.,* 531n., 536f., 510f.
6. *Ibid.,* 527ff. *FRUSV-64,* 179-82.
7. Schlesinger, *Bitter Heritage*; see *APNM*, ch. 4. On the PR function of staged elections in Vietnam and elsewhere, see Herman and Brodhead,

Demonstration Elections; MC, ch. 3.

8. Schlesinger, *RFK*, 734, 739.
9. See *FRS*, 25.
10. Howard Zinn and I were the applicants; the chapter was Arlington, near Cambridge. The details are not without interest.
11. On media coverage of the war from the early 1950s through 1985, see *MC*, 169-296 and App. 3.
12. Lewis and others, see *MC*, 170f. Kann, *WSJ*, Sept. 9, 1992. Michael Elliott, *BG*, Oct. 27, 1991. *G&M*, Feb. 27, 1992.
13. See *MC*, ch. 5.5.2, App. 3.
14. Brown, *JFK*, 34ff.
15. O'Donnell, *Johnny*, cited by Newman, *JFK and Vietnam*, 322f. Also Schlesinger, *RFK*, 711-2.
16. Newman, *JFK*, 324; Schlesinger, *RFK*, 712. Note that withdrawal had begun a month earlier, with ample publicity. Possibly Mansfield had forgotten.
17. Paterson, *Kennedy's Quest*, 21. *FRUSV*, IV 254,192 (167), 281.
18. Sorenson, *Kennedy Legacy*, 204-8; also *Kennedy*, 657.
19. Schlesinger, *RFK*, ch. 31. Chapter 32 is devoted to RFK and Vietnam in the post-assassination years, with a look backwards as well.
20. See note 1.
21. Schlesinger refers to Hilsman's hawkish August 30, 1963 memorandum, omitting its most inflammatory content (*RFK*, 720; see p. 40-41, above). He reports Hilsman's private statement to him discounting it as a response to a query by Rusk that offered "the whole range of *possible* responses." The document in fact proposes a *single* "U.S. Response" to each of the "Possible Diem-Nhu moves," each such response having several components; they are not presented as alternatives, indeed could not be, given the wording.
22. *1000 Days*, 902-3.
23. Review of Newman (see ch. 1, n. 39); *1000 Days*, 825. On Schlesinger's review, see *LL*, letter 17.
24. *RFK*, 701; Ball, *Past*, 364.
25. Review of Newman.
26. *RFK*, 725f.
27. In both, the word "object" appears instead of "objective."
28. *RFK*, 728-9.
29. Hilsman, letter, *NYT*, Jan. 20; *TLS*, April 3, 1992 (responding to Grenier; *cf.* note 1); letter, *Tikkun*, Summer 1992.
30. *Ibid.* The "news conference" appears to be the Cronkite TV interview; *To Move a Nation*, 497, where the wording is given slightly differently.
31. Kuttner, *BG*, Jan. 17, 1993. Shapley, *Promise*, 262f.
32. Colby, jacket cover. On the reaction to Newman's "examination of documents" by the first historian to check his files, see ch. 1, n. 92.
33. Newman, *JFK*, 457, 127, 180, 49. See p. 367 for a sample of Taylor's

alleged treachery.

34. *Ibid.*, 141, 137, 154, 147.
35. *Ibid.*, 285f., 319f., 290-1. *FRUSV,* III 518f.
36. Newman, *JFK,* 410, 321-4.
37. *Ibid.*, 423f.
38. *Ibid.*, 15f.
39. *Ibid.*, 71f., 88ff., 93, 67f.
40. *Ibid.*, 355-6. *FRUSV,* IV 74.
41. Newman, *JFK,* 448-9; Kamow, *Vietnam,* 326. Newman on Kamow, *BG,* Jan. 14, 1992. Newman's references are often unreliable. Another example is a discussion (408) of John Mecklin's reaction to the official statement on the McNamara-Taylor proposal of October 1963, which he found "sickening" at first but later came to see as a "brilliantly realistic and imaginative" White House plan; in context, the citation gives the impression that Mecklin recognized]FK's plan for "genuine withdrawal," whereas he was in fact discussing the "compromise" of a "politician...between the two U.S. factions" that differed on how best to pressure Diem. Similarly, Newman makes much of the fact that on Nov. 12, 1963, Kennedy said only that we should stay on in Vietnam until South Vietnam can maintain itself "as a free and independent country," permitting "democratic forces within the country to operate"; this comes close to advocating political settlement, Newman states, reflecting the President's intention to withdraw. Virtually the same statement, also implying nothing of the sort, opens NSAM 52, May 11, 1961 (426; *PP,* II 642). There are many other examples.
42. Newman, *JFK,* 236, 254.
43. *Ibid.*, 351f. *FRUSV,* I 638f., Aug. 26; IV 4f., Aug. 28 (see p. 40, above).
44. Newman, *JFK,* 410, 423-5, 435.
45. *Ibid.*, 410, 325, 403, 387, 359.
46. Thus Newman traces the planning of "South Vietnamese operations against North Vietnam" to May 1963, the "seed" for what became OPLAN 34A "and the secret American actions that led to the Gulf of Tonkin incidents in August 1964." The seeds "sprouted in the November 20 [1963] Honolulu meeting"; plans were "scaled back" in the draft prepared for Kennedy, but "the dam broke when NSAM-273 was rewritten" and adopted on Nov. 26, "the most significant of all the changes" made to the draft (375f., 446f.). This is mostly incorrect. As discussed earlier, covert operations against the North had been underway since mid-1962, apparently with US and third country participation, and appear in the internal record from Jan. 1963, endorsed in April by Hilsman. NSAM 273 is not different in any relevant way from the draft. Furthermore, the record shows no increased US participation in OPLAN 34A to the Tonkin Gulf incident (in fact, denies it), though DE SOTO intelligence patrols were then underway.
47. Letter, *NYT,* March 23, 1992.

48. Newman, *BG*, Jan. 14; *JFK*, 409-10; letter, *Nation*, May l8, 1992.

49. Prouty, *JFK*, xviii.

50. Dallas speech cited by Paterson, *Kennedy's Quest*; Raskin, *op. cit.*, from *Public Papers of the Presidents*. Du Boff, *Accumulation*, 101. Heller cited by Richard Du Boff and Edward Herman, "The New Economics and the Contradictions of Keynesianism," *Review of Radical Political Economics*, URPE, Aug. 1972. On these matters, see MacDougall, *Heavens*.

51. See *DD*, 26; *501*, ch. 3, n. 12.

52. Bundy, *Danger*, 460-1.

53. Jeffreys-Jones, *CIA*; Ranelagh, *Agency*. See also Blum, *CIA*.

54. Hilsman, *To Move a Nation*, 85f.

55. Spears, in Jeffreys-Jones and Lownie, *North American Spies*.

56. Du Boff and Herman, *op. cit.*; Du Boff, *Accumulation*, 101.

57. Paterson, in Paterson, *Kennedy's Quest*; Garthoff, *Détente*, 80; McClintock, *Instruments*, 207, 205. See *NI*, 274-5. On JFK's terror against Cuba, see Hinckle & Turner, *Deadly Secrets*. Missile Crisis, see *501*, 148.

58. Rabe, in Paterson, *Kennedy's Quest*. Nairn, *Progressive*, May 1984. See *TTT*, *501*, and sources cited; Walter LaFeber, "The Alliances in Retrospect," in Maguire and Brown, *Bordering*; Williams, *Export Agriculture*. Kennedy and Brazil, *501*, ch. 7.3. On "economic miracles," see *501*, ch. 7.

59. Bowles, Oral History; Kennedy, *Public Papers of the Presidents*, 1961, cited by Paterson, *op. cit.*, 19, 136. See *TTT*, ch. 4.

60. See *501*, ch. 11.

Bibliography

Ball, George. *The Past has another Pattern* (Norton, 1982)

Bergerud, Eric. *The Dynamics of Defeat* (Westview, 1991)

Berman, Larry. *Planning a Tragedy* (Norton, 1982)

Blum, William. *The CIA: a forgotten history* (Zed Books, 1986)

Brown, Thomas. *JFK: History of an Image* (Indiana, 1988)

Browne, Malcolm. *The New Face of War* (Bobbs-Merrill, 1965)

Bundy, McGeorge. *Danger and Survival* (Random House, 1988)

Chomsky, Noam. *American Power and the New Mandarins* (Pantheon, 1969) [*APNM*]

———. *At War with Asia* (Pantheon, 1970) [*AWWA*]

———. *For Reasons of State* (Pantheon, 1973) [*FRS*]

———. *Turning the Tide* (South End Press, 1985) [*TIT*]

———. *Necessary Illusions* (South End Press, 1989) [*NI*]

———. *Deterring Democracy* (Verso, 1991; updated edition, Hill &Wang, 1992) [*DO*]

———. *Year 501* (South End Press, 1993) [*501*]

———. *Letters from Lexington: Reflections on Propaganda* (Common Courage, 1993) [*LL*]

———, and Edward Herman. *Political Economy of Human Rights* (South End Press, 1979) [*PEHR*]

———, and Howard Zinn, eds. *Pentagon Papers*, vol. 5, Analytic Essays and Index (Beacon Press, 1972) [*PP V*]

Cooper, Chester. *The Lost Crusade* (Dodd, Mead, 1970)

Cumings, Bruce. *The Origins of the Korean War*, vol. II (Princeton, 1990)

Drinnon, Richard. *Facing West: The Metaphysics of Indian-Hating and Empire-Building* (Minnesota, 1980)

Du Boff, Richard. *Accumulation and Power* (ME Sharpe, 1989)

Duffy, Dan, ed. *Informed Dissent* (Vietnam Generation, Burning Cities Press, 1992)

Duncanson, Denis. *Government and Revolution in Vietnam* (Oxford, 1968)

Fall, Bernard. *Last Reflections on War* (Doubleday, 1967)

———, and Marcus Raskin, eds. *Vietnam Reader* (Vintage, 1965)

197

Garthoff, Raymond. *Reflections on the Cuban Missile Crisis* (Brookings, 1987)
Gibbon, William Conrad, ed. *The U.S. Government and the Vietnam War,* part II, 1961-1964 (Princeton, 1986)
Giglio, James. *The Presidency of John F. Kennedy* (Kansas, 1991)
Griffen, William, and John Marciano. *Lessons of the Vietnam War: A Critical Examination of School Texts* (Rowman and Allanheld, 1979)
Herman, Edward. *The Real Terror Network* (South End Press, 1982)
———, and Frank Brodhead. *Demonstration Elections* (South End, 1984)
———, and Noam Chomsky. *Manufacturing Consent* (Pantheon, 1988) [MC]
Hilsman, Roger. *To Move a Nation* (Dell, 1967)
Hinckle, Warren, and William Turner. *Deadly Secrets* (Thunder's Mouth, 1992)
Horsman, Reginald. *Expansion and American Indian Policy* (Michigan State, 1967)
Jeffreys-Jones, Rhodri. *The CIA & American Democracy* (Yale, 1989)
———, and Andrew Lownie, eds. *North American Spies* (Edinburgh, 1992)
Kahin, George. *Intervention* (Knopf, 1986)
Karnow, Stanley. *Vietnam, A History* (Viking, 1983)
Kennan, George F. *Russia Leaves the War* (Princeton, 1956)
Kiernan, V.G. *The Lords of Human Kind* (Columbia, 1986)
Kinnard, Douglas. *The War Managers* (University Press of New England, 1977)
Kolko, Gabriel. *Anatomy of a War* (Pantheon, 1985)
Leffler, Michael. *A Preponderance of Power* (Stanford, 1992)
Lewy, Guenter. *America in Vietnam* (Oxford, 1978)
Maguire, Andrew, and Janet W. Brown, eds. *Bordering on Trouble* (Adler & Adler, 1986)
McClintock, Michael. *Instruments of Statecraft* (Pantheon, 1992)
McDougall, Walter. *...the Heavens and the Earth* (Basic Books, 1985)
Mowlana, Hamid, George Gerbner, and Herbert Schiller. *Triumph of the Image* (Westview, 1992)
Newman, John. *JFK and Vietnam: Deception, Intrigue, and the Struggle for Power* (Warner, 1992)
O'Donnell, Kenneth, and David Powers. *"Johnny, We Hardly Knew Ye"* (Little, Brown, 1972)
Paterson, Thomas, ed. *Kennedy's Quest for Victory* (Oxford, 1989)
Prouty, Fletcher. *JFK* (Birch Lane, 1992)
Race, Jeffrey. *War Comes to Long An* (California, 1971)
Ranelagh, John. *The Agency* (Simon &: Schuster, 1986)
Schlesinger, Arthur. *A Thousand Days* (Houghton Mifflin, 1965; Fawcett, 1967)
———. *The Bitter Heritage* (Houghton Mifflin, 1966)
———. *Robert Kennedy and His Times* (Houghton Mifflin, 1978)
Shaplen, Robert. *The Lost Revolution* (Harper & Row, 1965)

Shapley, Deborah. *Promise and Power* (Little, Brown, 1993)

Simpson, Christopher. *The Splendid Blond Beast* (Grove, 1993)

Sorenson, Theodore. *Kennedy* (Harper & Row, 1965)

——. *The Kennedy Legacy* (MacMillan, 1969)

Taylor, Maxwell. *Swords and Plowshares* (Norton, 1972)

Tregaskis, Richard. *Vietnam Diary* (Holt, Rinehart & Winston, 1963)

Tsou, Tang, ed. *China in Crisis* (Chicago, 1968), vol. II

US Government, Department of State. *Foreign Relations of the United States, Vietnam, 1961-1963* [*FRUSV*], vols. I-IV

——. *Foreign Relations of the United States, Vietnam, 1964-1968*, vol. I [*FRUSV-64*]

——, Dept. of Defense. *Pentagon Papers*, Gravel edition (Beacon, 1971) [*PP*]; 4 volumes. Fifth volume of analytic essays and index, 1972

Vickery, Michael. *Cambodia: 1975-1982* (South End Press, 1984)

Weeks, William Earl. *John Quincy Adams and American Global Empire* (Kentucky, 1992)

Westing, Arthur H. *Herbicides in War* (SIPRI; Taylor & Francis, 1984)

Williams, Robert. *Export Agriculture and the Crisis in Central America* (North Carolina, 1986)

Yergin, Daniel. *Shattered Peace* (Houghton Mifflin, 1977)

Zinn, Howard. *Vietnam: The Logic of Withdrawal* (Beacon, 1967)

Index

About the Author

© Don Usner

Noam Chomsky is widely regarded as one of the foremost critics of US foreign policy in the world. He has published numerous groundbreaking books, articles, and essays on global politics, history, and linguistics. Among his recent books are *Masters of Mankind* and *Hopes and Prospects*. This book is part of a collection of twelve new editions from Haymarket Books of Chomsky's classic works.